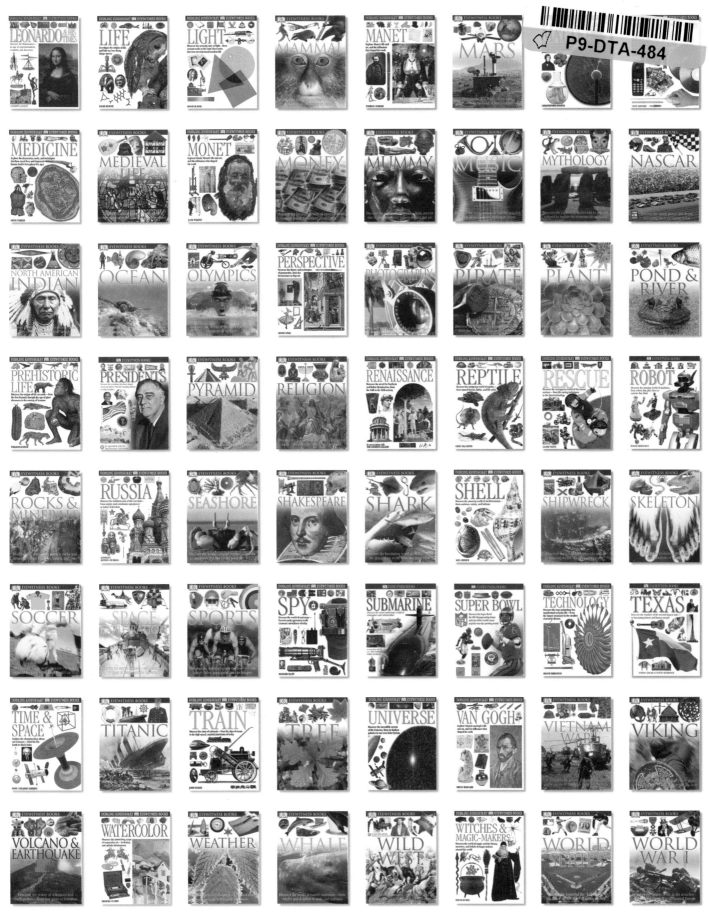

Eyewitness
EXPLORER

Sealskin hood and mitten from Arctic expedition 1875–1876

Shoot and bark from *chinchona* plant from which quinine is obtained

Map showing Phoenicia on the eastern coast of the Mediterranean

Inca beaker brought back by Francisco Pizarro

Captain Meriwether Lewis

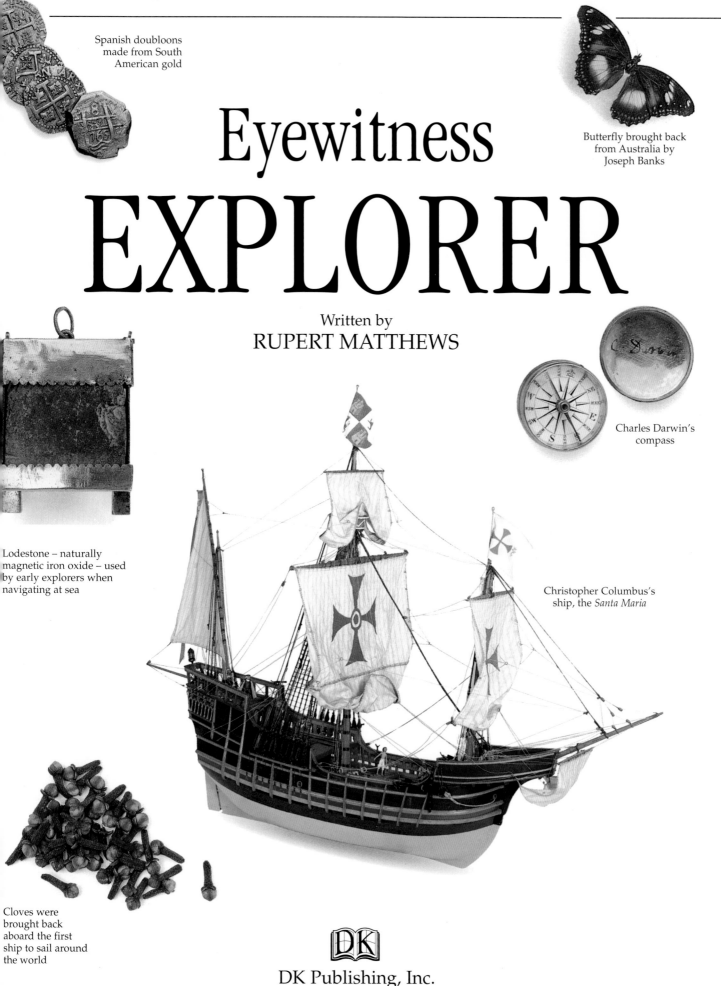

Spanish doubloons
made from South
American gold

Butterfly brought back
from Australia by
Joseph Banks

Eyewitness
EXPLORER

Written by
RUPERT MATTHEWS

Charles Darwin's
compass

Lodestone – naturally
magnetic iron oxide – used
by early explorers when
navigating at sea

Christopher Columbus's
ship, the *Santa Maria*

Cloves were
brought back
aboard the first
ship to sail around
the world

DK

DK Publishing, Inc.

Indian wooden
mask presented to
Charles Wilkes and
Meriwether Lewis

**LONDON, NEW YORK, MUNICH,
MELBOURNE, and DELHI**

Viking gold rings
found in Ireland

Project editor Linda Martin
Art editor Alison Anholt-White
Senior editor Helen Parker
Senior art editor Julia Harris
Production Louise Barratt
Picture research Kathy Lockley

Special photograpy
James Stevenson, Tina Chambers, Keith Percival,
Barrie Cash of the National Maritime Museum, London;
Alan Hills, Ivor Curzlake, Philip Nicholls and Chas Howson
of the British Museum, London

REVISED EDITION
Managing editor Andrew Macintyre
Managing art editor Jane Thomas
Category publisher Linda Martin
Art director Simon Webb
Editor and reference compiler Sue Nicholson
Art editor Andrew Nash
Production Jenny Jacoby
Picture research Deborah Pownall
DTP designer Siu Yin Ho

U.S. editors Elizabeth Hester, John Searcy
Publishing director Beth Sutinis
Art director Dirk Kaufman
U.S. DTP designer Milos Orlovic
U.S. production Chris Avgherinos, Ivor Parker

This Eyewitness ® Guide has been conceived by
Dorling Kindersley Limited and Editions Gallimard

This edition published in the United States in 2005
by DK Publishing, Inc.
375 Hudson Street, New York, NY 10014

05 06 07 08 09 10 9 8 7 6 5 4 3 2

Copyright © 1991, © 2005, Dorling Kindersley Limited

A catalog record for this book is
available from the Library of Congress.

ISBN 0-7566-1071-0 (HC) 0-7566-1072-9 (Library Binding)

Color reproduction by
Colourscan, Singapore
Printed in China by Toppan Printing Co.,
(Shenzen) Ltd.

Discover more at
www.dk.com

Inuit (Eskimo)
bone knives

Banjo taken on
Ernest
Shackleton's
Antarctic
expedition

Contents

Henry Stanley's hat

6
Early explorers

8
Egyptian expeditions

10
Imperial expansion

12
Viking voyages

14
Polynesian settlers

16
The Silk Road

18
Arab adventurers

20
The Age of Exploration

22
The New World

24
Around the world

26
Life at sea

28
Tricks of the trade

30
Gold and the gospel

34
The Great South Sea

36
The Endeavour

38
Across Australia

40
The Northwest Passage

42
North America tamed

46
The Dark Continent

48
Naturalist explorers

52
The North Pole

54
The South Pole

56
Pioneers of the air

58
Into outer space

60
Exploring the deep

62
Exploration routes

64
Did you know?

66
Timeline of explorers

68
Find out more

70
Glossary

72
Index

Early explorers

SIX THOUSAND YEARS AGO people knew little of what existed more than a few days' journey away from their own homes. Because they could grow all their own food and make everything they needed, they had no need to travel far. However, as civilization developed, so did the idea of trading goods with other countries. One of the earliest peoples to begin trading were the Phoenicians, who lived in cities on the Mediterranean coast of what is now Israel and Lebanon. The Phoenicians were expert shipbuilders and were able to sail great distances. They also realized that they couldmake money by trading. Between about 1100 B.C. and 700 B.C., Phoenician ships explored the entire Mediterranean, searching for new markets and establishing colonies. They even sailed through the Strait of Gibraltar to the Atlantic, and reached Britain and West Africa.

GLASS BEADS
Phoenician craftsmen were expert glass workers and were able to produce intricate pieces that were then sold abroad. This necklace was found in a tomb on the site of the ancient city of Tharros in Sardinia.

Demon head

Disk representing the world

Carthaginian coin from Spain

Copper coin from Cádiz

Silver coin from Carthage

EARLY MAP
This clay tablet was found in Iraq and shows the earliest-known map of the world. The world is surrounded by an ever-flowing stream, the "Bitter River."

COINS
Early Phoenician merchants swapped goods, but later traders used coins – pieces of metal stamped to show their origin.

Burial urn

Underground cellars

Phoenician inscription

BURIAL URN
This urn, found in Carthage, North Africa (near present-day Tunis), contains the bones of a child. Carthage was the main trading center for all Phoenician colonies. It was the custom there to sacrifice children to gods and goddesses; the bones were then buried in pottery burial urns in underground cellars.

BROKEN POTTERY
This piece of broken pottery is inscribed in Phoenician with the name of the powerful and beautiful goddess Astarte. It was found on the island of Malta, which lay on several shipping routes. Malta was colonized by the Phoenicians as a trading center.

118537

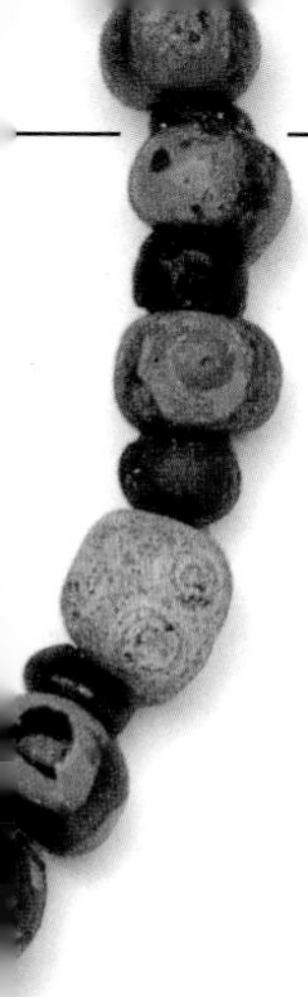

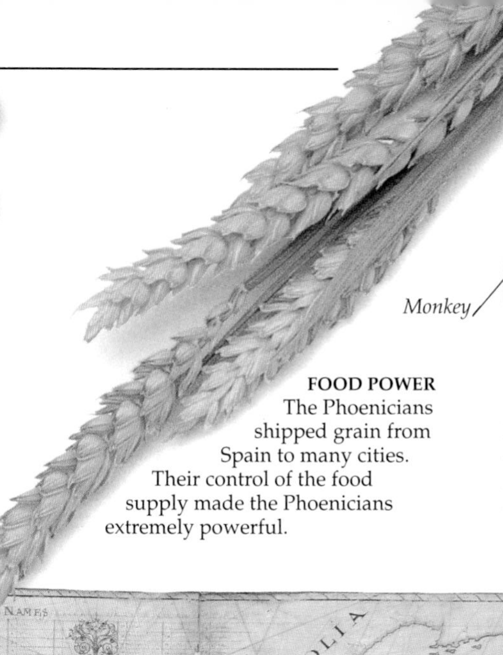

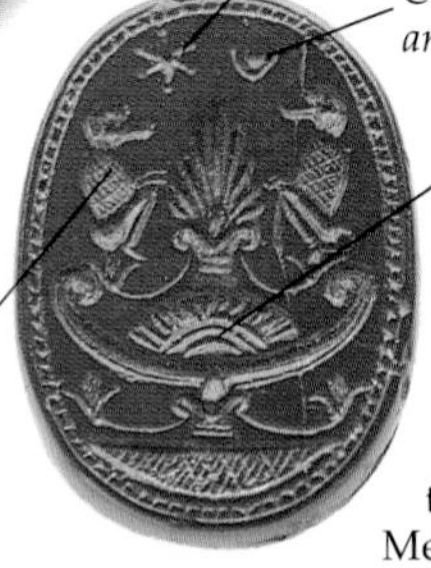

FOOD POWER
The Phoenicians shipped grain from Spain to many cities. Their control of the food supply made the Phoenicians extremely powerful.

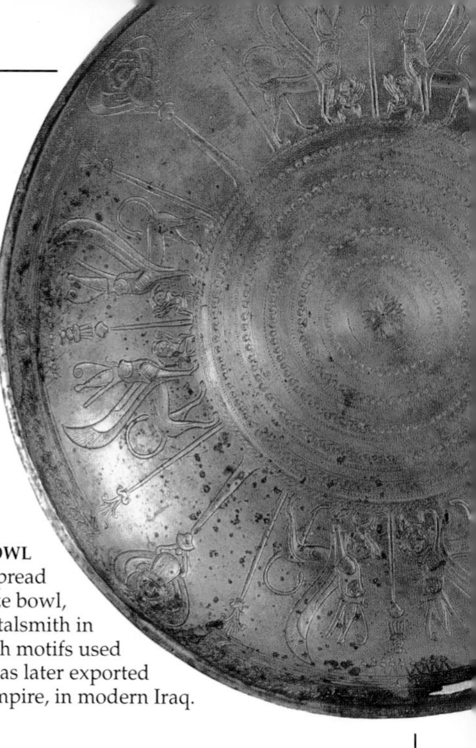

JASPER SEAL
Ornamental seals were favorite items throughout the Mediterranean. High-quality pieces like this were carved by Phoenician craftsmen from jasper mined in Sardinia, and shipped elsewhere for sale.

Star

Crescent and disk

Lotus flower

Monkey

BRONZE BOWL
Phoenician trade helped to spread culture and ideas. This bronze bowl, made by a Phoenician metalsmith in about 750 B.C., is decorated with motifs used by the Egyptians. It was later exported to the Assyrian Empire, in modern Iraq.

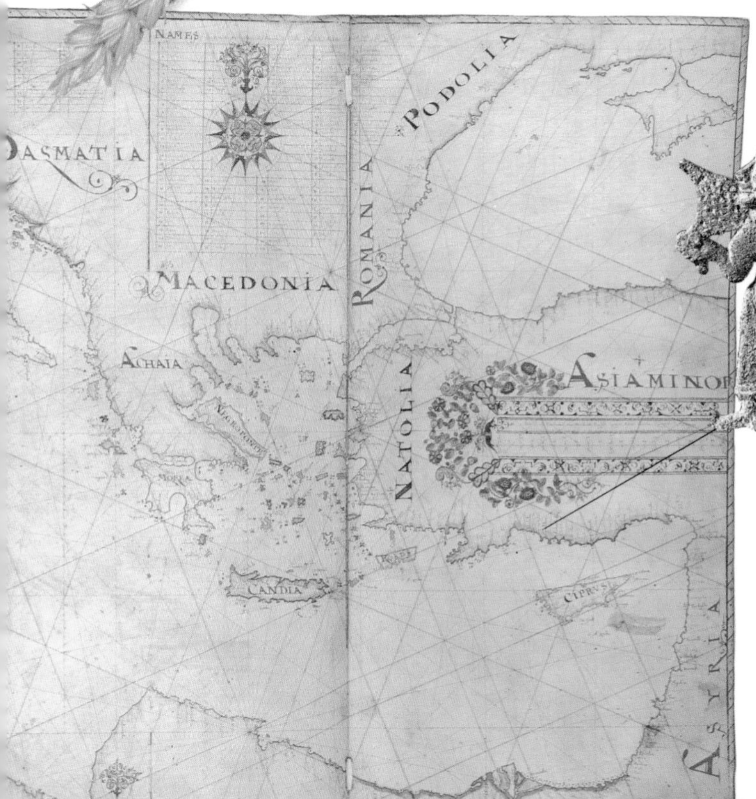

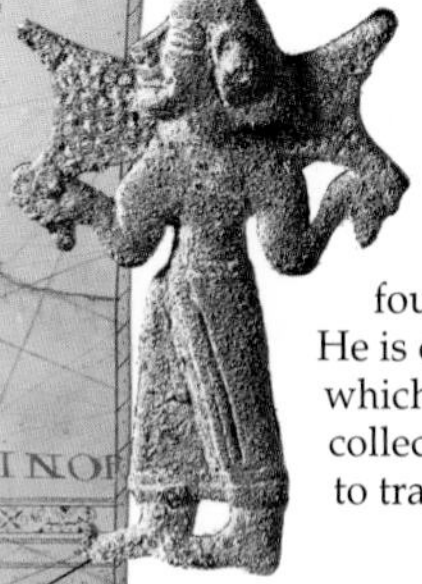

COPPER CARRIER
This figure of a Phoenician merchant was found on Cyprus. He is carrying copper, which the Phoenicians collected from Cyprus to trade elsewhere.

WESTWARD BOUND
The Phoenicians dominated trade and exploration in the Mediterranean for several hundred years. As you can see from this map, they sailed westward from their homeland in the Middle East, finding new peoples with whom to trade goods.

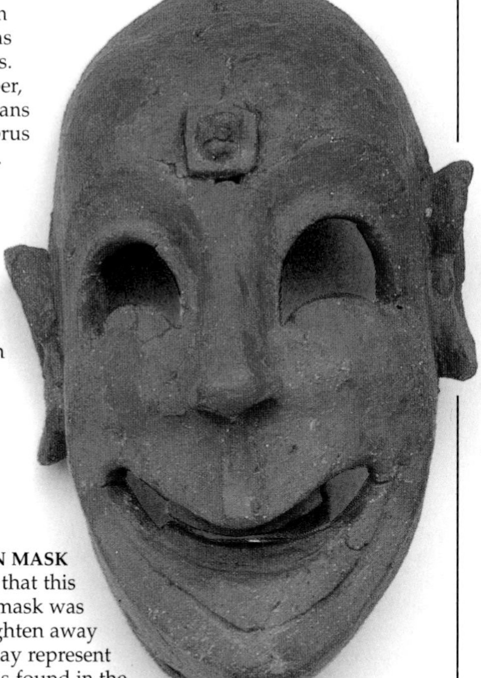

DEMON MASK
It is thought that this terracotta mask was intended to frighten away evil spirits. It may represent a demon and was found in the tomb of a Phoenician on the island of Sardinia in the Mediterranean.

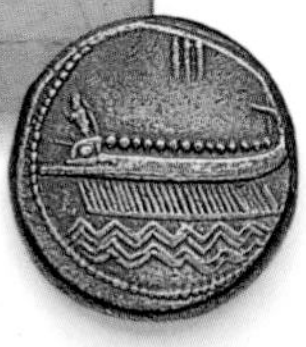

BALAWAT GATES *below*
This bronze plaque from a pair of gates was found at Balawat in Iraq. It depicts Phoenician officials leaving Tyre. The king and queen (left) watch them as they set sail.

Silver coin from Sidon showing a Phoenician galley (ship)

Gates of Tyre

Loaded ships

Cargo being unloaded

Egyptian expeditions

THE WORLD'S EARLIEST CIVILIZATIONS, of which Egypt was one, developed in the rich lands of the Middle East. By 3000 B.C., Egypt had become a state, and numerous towns and cities sprang up in the fertile valley of the Nile River. According to Egyptian belief – as taught by the priests – the world was flat and rectangular; the heavens were supported by four massive pillars at each corner of the Earth, beyond which lay the Ocean – "a vast, endless stretch of ever-flowing water." At first, the Egyptians stayed in the Nile Valley, but they soon began traveling farther and farther in search of new peoples to trade with. One of the most famous Egyptian voyages was made to Punt at the command of Queen Hatshepsut (see below). Despite this expedition, Egyptian priests still asserted the existence of sky supports – they were just farther away than the priests thought!

REED BOATS
Before the Egyptians found cedar wood for building ocean-going boats, sailing was restricted to the Nile River. Nile boats were made from reeds lashed together to form a slightly concave (inward-curving) structure.

ROYAL CARTOUCHE
A cartouche is an oval shape in which characters representing a sovereign's name are written. This is the cartouche of Queen Hatshepsut.

Faience

BEETLE RINGS
Egyptian rings were often made with a stone shaped like a scarab beetle. These scarab rings carry the cartouche of Queen Hatshepsut and belonged to her officials. They are made of gold, faience (glazed ware), and lapis lazuli that was imported from other lands.

Lapis lazuli

QUEEN HATSHEPSUT
Around 1490 B.C., Queen Hatshepsut sent a fleet of ships southward through the Red Sea, and possibly as far as the Indian Ocean. The expedition found a country called Punt (probably modern-day Somalia, East Africa), where they were delighted to find ivory, ebony, and myrrh trees.

WOODEN SHIP *below*
After about 2700 B.C., the Egyptians began building wooden sailing ships capable of sea voyages. These ships sailed along the Mediterranean coasts to trade with nearby countries.

Bow (front of ship)

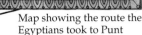

Map showing the route the Egyptians took to Punt

PRETTY FACES
Egyptian nobility wore large amounts of make-up, which they kept in containers such as this. Merchants explored many areas of North Africa and western Asia searching for cosmetic ingredients.

Thick rope pulled tight to stop the boat from sagging at each end

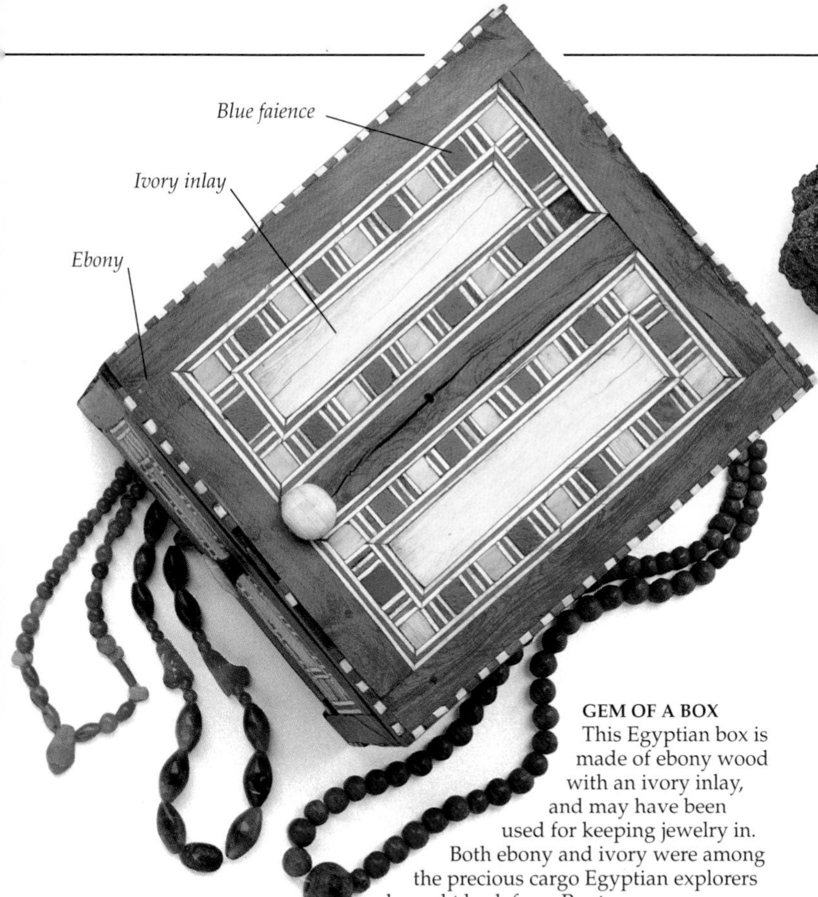

Blue faience

Ivory inlay

Ebony

Myrrh gum resin

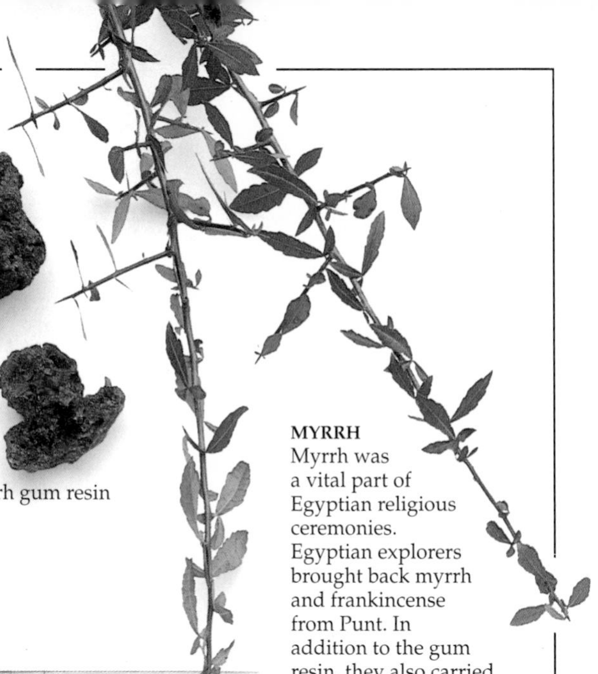

MYRRH
Myrrh was
a vital part of
Egyptian religious
ceremonies.
Egyptian explorers
brought back myrrh
and frankincense
from Punt. In
addition to the gum
resin, they also carried
back myrrh trees to
plant in front of Queen
Hatshepsut's temple.

GEM OF A BOX
This Egyptian box is
made of ebony wood
with an ivory inlay,
and may have been
used for keeping jewelry in.
Both ebony and ivory were among
the precious cargo Egyptian explorers
brought back from Punt.

This copy of a tomb
painting shows
Egyptians making
piles of incense

Pellets
burned here

Container for
pellets of incense

BRONZE BURNER
Incense, such as myrrh and frankincense, was
burned at all Egyptian religious ceremonies and
was very valuable. This bronze incense burner
has a falcon head, and it may have been sacred to
the sky god Horus.

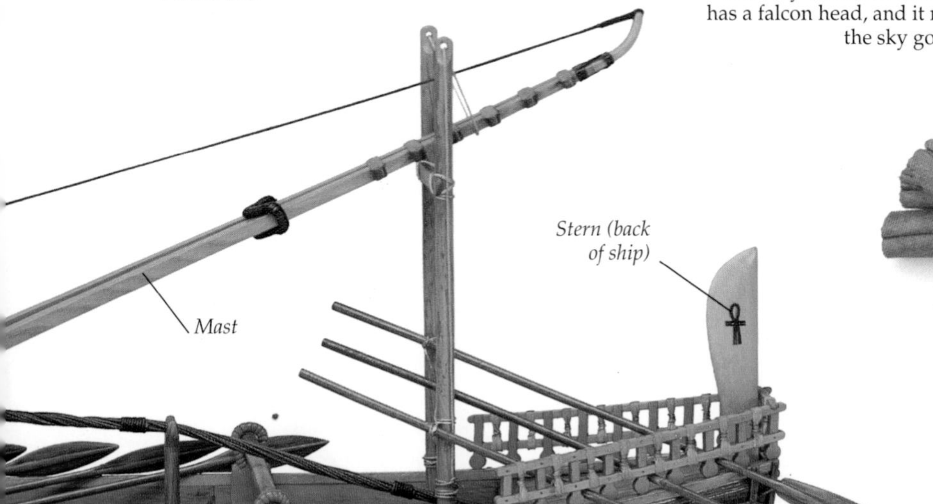

Falcon head

Cinnamon sticks

Mast

Stern (back
of ship)

SAUCY SPICES
Cinnamon spice was often
used in cooking by rich Egyptians. It came from
the coast of India; from there it was shipped by
Arabs to Arabia (pp. 18–19) for sale to Egyptian
merchants.

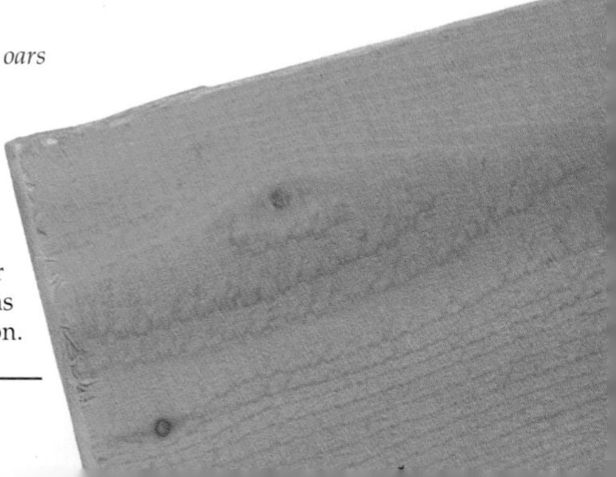

Steering oars

STRONG CEDAR
Sea-going ships like the one on
the left were built from cedar
wood, which the Egyptians
brought back from Lebanon.

Imperial expansion

JASON AND THE ARGONAUTS
The ancient Greek legends of Jason – a heroic sailor who voyaged to many distant countries – were almost certainly romanticized accounts of real Greek journeys of exploration.

THE MEDITERRANEAN WAS dominated by two great empires during the period between about 350 B.C. and A.D. 500. Alexander the Great, king of Macedonia (now part of northern Greece), conquered a vast empire which stretched from Greece to Egypt to India. The later Roman Empire was even larger, reaching from northern Britain to the Sahara desert in Africa, and from the Black Sea to the Atlantic Ocean. It was a time of great exploration and expansion, both on land and sea.
Alexander sent ambassadors to the distant lands of northern India to establish contacts. Roman emperors sent many expeditions both into Europe and into Africa. Much exploration, however, was undertaken by private merchants and travelers; some evidence of their activities can be seen on these pages. One Greek merchant is said to have sailed to Iceland in search of new lands, and Romans traded with the wandering nomad peoples of Central Asia.

Alexander sent peacocks from India back to Greece

THE HAWK
This gold Greek brooch was found in Ephesus, an ancient Greek city just south of present-day Izmir in Turkey.

TRADING SOUTH
This small stone baboon was found on the site of Naucratis, a Greek colony in the Nile Delta. The colony was founded in about 540 B.C. by Greek merchants who traded for spices from Arabia and for ivory from Africa.

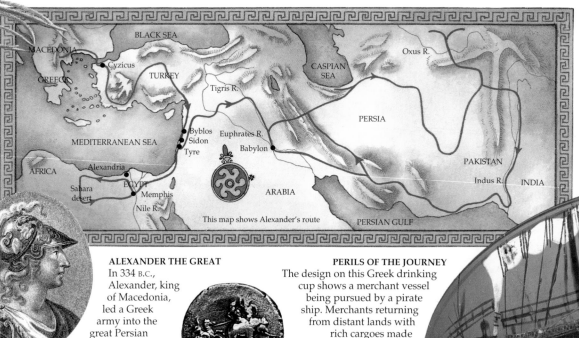

This map shows Alexander's route

ALEXANDER THE GREAT
In 334 B.C., Alexander, king of Macedonia, led a Greek army into the great Persian Empire. By 327 B.C., he had captured an area that stretched from Egypt in the west to the Indus River, Pakistan, in the east. The following year, he conquered parts of northern India before returning to Persia. His vast empire allowed Greek merchants and travelers to penetrate deep into Asia.

This coin shows Alexander attacking an Indian king

PERILS OF THE JOURNEY
The design on this Greek drinking cup shows a merchant vessel being pursued by a pirate ship. Merchants returning from distant lands with rich cargoes made easy prey.

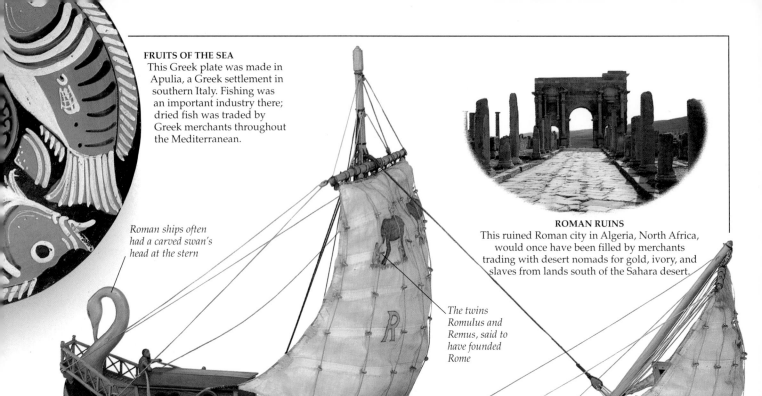

FRUITS OF THE SEA
This Greek plate was made in Apulia, a Greek settlement in southern Italy. Fishing was an important industry there; dried fish was traded by Greek merchants throughout the Mediterranean.

ROMAN RUINS
This ruined Roman city in Algeria, North Africa, would once have been filled by merchants trading with desert nomads for gold, ivory, and slaves from lands south of the Sahara desert.

Roman ships often had a carved swan's head at the stern

The twins Romulus and Remus, said to have founded Rome

Steering oar

Roman glass bowl

TRADING EXPLORERS
The Roman silver cup on the right was found in Britain and is thought to have been imported by Roman traders – the first Romans other than Caesar's soldiers to explore Britain. The glass bowl on the left was found in the eastern Mediterranean.

ROMAN MERCHANT SHIP
Merchant ships of the Roman Empire had two masts and a wide cargo hold. Such ships could not sail against the wind and were only put to sea when the wind was favorable. These ships brought back wild animals from Africa to fight Roman gladiators; they also carried rich cargoes of gems, spices, and silk from Asia (pp. 16–17).

Indian coin

Arabian coin

FOREIGN IMITATIONS
Roman influence spread far beyond the Empire's frontiers. These coins carry Roman designs, but were actually minted in Arabia and India.

Roman silver cup

CAESAR IN FRANCE
This Roman coin was made in the Roman colony of Vienne, in southern France, around 36 B.C. The letters "CI V" stand for "Colonia Julia Viennensis" (the "Colony of Julius Caesar at Vienne").

Prow of Roman ship

Viking voyages

ERIC THE RED
Eric was a typical Viking explorer. He left Norway with his father who was escaping trial for murder, and settled in Iceland. After killing a rival settler there, Eric set sail to the west and found a land with fertile coastal plains which he called "Greenland." He persuaded many Vikings to settle there.

FAT SHIP
Vikings used *knorrs* when on trading voyages or migrating to new lands. *Knorrs* were wide-bellied ships, which meant they had room for passengers and cargo. They were also shallow in depth, which enabled Viking sailors to take them upriver, far inland.

Europe was seldom free from the menace of ruthless Viking raiders during the early Middle Ages. From the 8th to the 12th century, boatloads of Vikings left their Scandinavian homeland on voyages of exploration. The motives for these journeys were varied. Some Vikings were interested only in stealing treasure and capturing slaves – they plundered and pillaged the unfortunate communities they found in Britain and the Mediterranean. But others were prompted to search for new lands across the Atlantic where they could settle, as farming land in Scandinavia was scarce. The Swedish Vikings, who were mainly traders, set their sights on the lands of Eastern Europe and Asia, with hopes of developing new trading markets. After about 1200, the Vikings became more settled and ceased their long voyages of discovery.

Steering oar

LAND AHOY!
Erik the Red's son, Leif Erikson, left Greenland in 1001 to investigate rumors of a land to the southwest. After an arduous voyage, he sighted a land of mountains and forests. This was Labrador, North America.

Steering oar

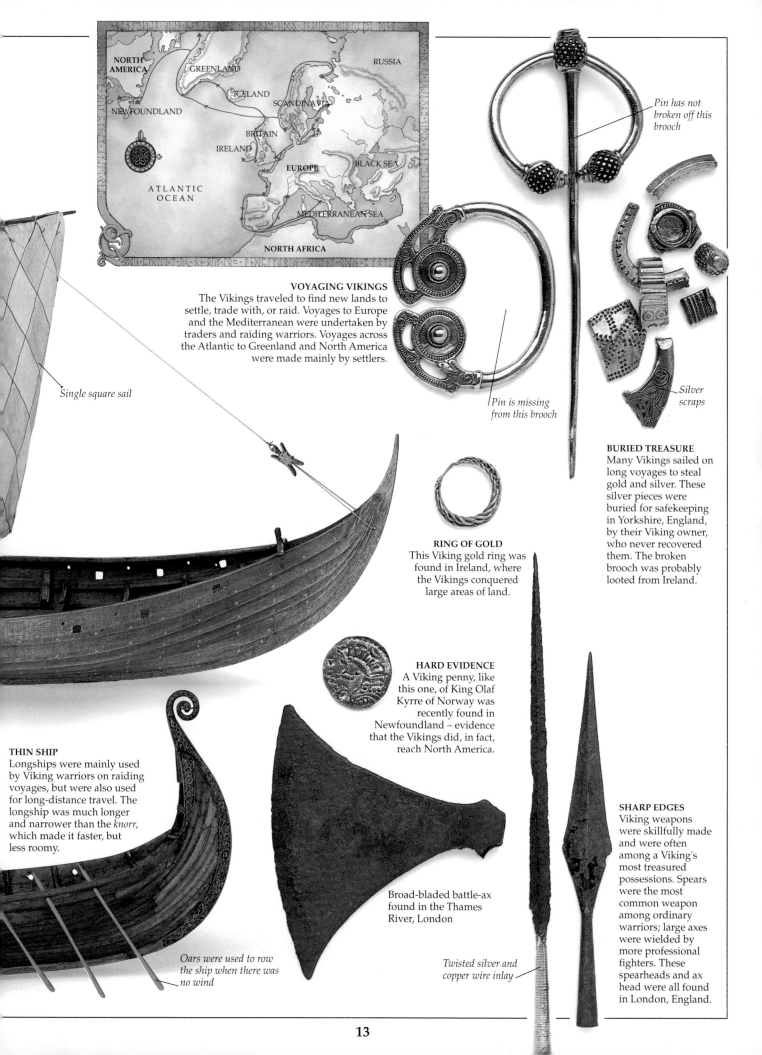

VOYAGING VIKINGS
The Vikings traveled to find new lands to settle, trade with, or raid. Voyages to Europe and the Mediterranean were undertaken by traders and raiding warriors. Voyages across the Atlantic to Greenland and North America were made mainly by settlers.

Single square sail

Pin has not broken off this brooch

Pin is missing from this brooch

Silver scraps

BURIED TREASURE
Many Vikings sailed on long voyages to steal gold and silver. These silver pieces were buried for safekeeping in Yorkshire, England, by their Viking owner, who never recovered them. The broken brooch was probably looted from Ireland.

RING OF GOLD
This Viking gold ring was found in Ireland, where the Vikings conquered large areas of land.

HARD EVIDENCE
A Viking penny, like this one, of King Olaf Kyrre of Norway was recently found in Newfoundland – evidence that the Vikings did, in fact, reach North America.

THIN SHIP
Longships were mainly used by Viking warriors on raiding voyages, but were also used for long-distance travel. The longship was much longer and narrower than the *knorr*, which made it faster, but less roomy.

Broad-bladed battle-ax found in the Thames River, London

Oars were used to row the ship when there was no wind

Twisted silver and copper wire inlay

SHARP EDGES
Viking weapons were skillfully made and were often among a Viking's most treasured possessions. Spears were the most common weapon among ordinary warriors; large axes were wielded by more professional fighters. These spearheads and ax head were all found in London, England.

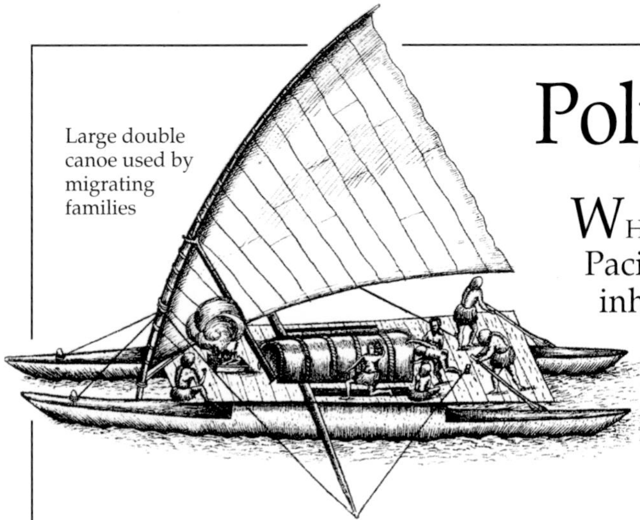

Large double canoe used by migrating families

Polynesian settlers

WHEN EUROPEANS FIRST REACHED the remote islands of the Pacific Ocean (pp. 62–63), they found the islands already inhabited by a people called the Polynesians. At about the same time as the Phoenicians were exploring the Mediterranean (pp. 6–7), the Polynesians were "island-hopping" thousands of miles eastward across the Pacific. These seafaring people traveled in relatively small canoes that were nevertheless strong and stable. They were expert seamen and navigators who could deduce the direction of land from the shape and size of waves and from the behavior of sea creatures. Historians think the main reason for these long voyages of exploration was to find new islands to colonize. The Polynesian population was a large one, and as one island became too crowded, some families would set off in search of the next island.

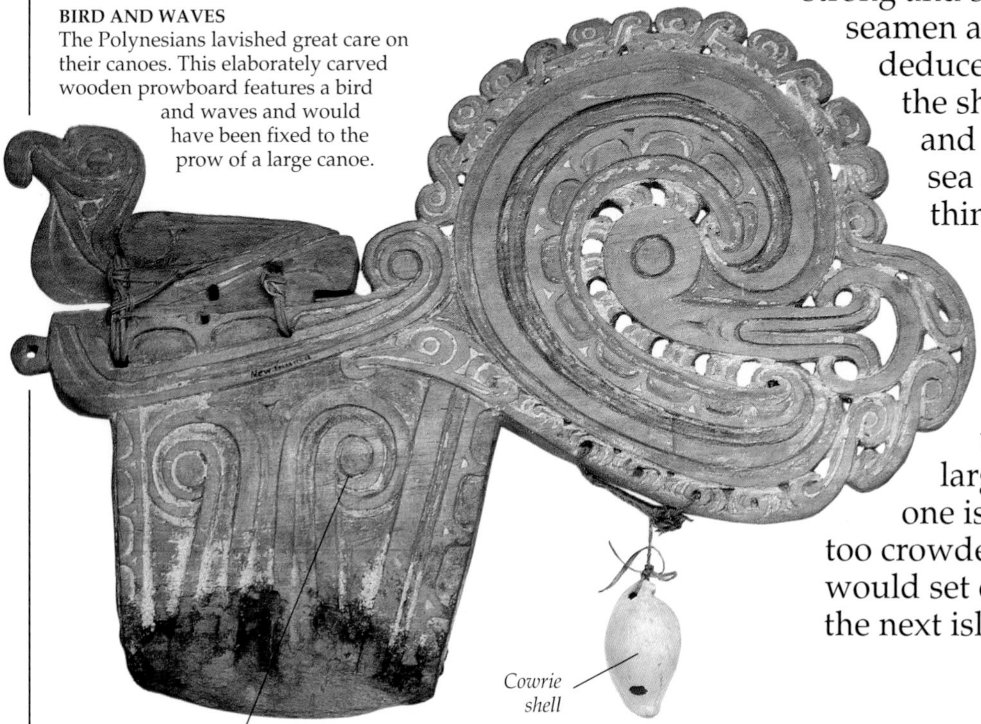

BIRD AND WAVES
The Polynesians lavished great care on their canoes. This elaborately carved wooden prowboard features a bird and waves and would have been fixed to the prow of a large canoe.

Cowrie shell

Waves

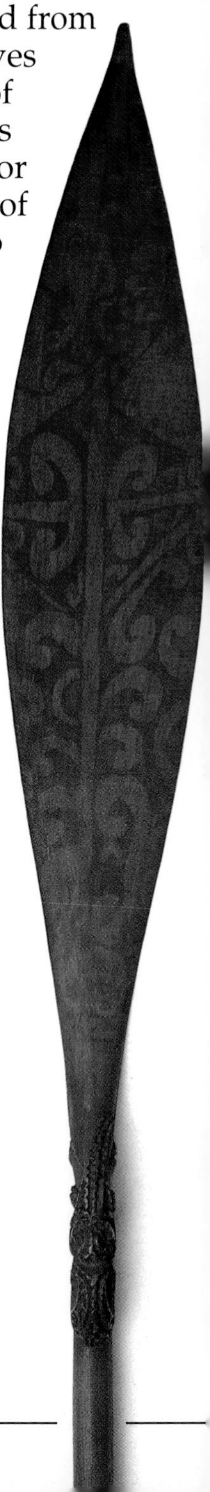

POLYNESIAN PADDLE
This finely carved canoe paddle comes from New Zealand. You can see paddles like this in use in the picture at the top of this page.

MODERN CANOE *left*
This modern racing canoe from Papua New Guinea (pp. 62–63) incorporates many features of the traditional Polynesian canoe. Though made of fiberglass, this canoe is the same shape and has a similar outrigger attached for stability.

SHORT-HAUL CANOE *below*
This model shows a small canoe such as those used by the Polynesians for fishing and for short voyages between neighboring islands. The main hull is made from a hollowed-out log, and the small outrigger adds stability by making the base of the canoe bigger.

Outrigger

LUCKY FISHING
The Polynesians believed that every occupation or place had its own god or spirit. This canoe god from the Cook Islands brought good luck to fishermen.

RELAXING BY THE SEA
European explorers found that the Polynesians enjoyed their warm and relaxing climate to the fullest!

Barbed point of spear was horribly effective

Polynesian spear

Human hair

Coconut fiber

SHELL NECKLACE
This necklace, made from shell, coconut fiber, and human hair, is also from the Cook Islands. Showy ornaments such as this were worn only by chiefs and their families.

Shell

WEAPONS OF WAR
Polynesians lived in a violent society. Warfare and feuding were common; sometimes quarrels continued from one generation to the next and claimed the lives of hundreds of people before they were forgotten. The weapons used by Polynesian warriors were simple, but brutally effective. Tribal armies fought with great discipline and courage, sometimes preferring annihilation (destruction) to the shame of surrender.

Polynesian war club

Shark's tooth

Hair

SWAYING SKIRT *above*
This Polynesian "grass" skirt is actually made from the inner bark of the hibiscus plant (pp. 50–51). Lightweight clothing like this was comfortable in the warm climate and allowed easy movement.

Fiji islander in dance costume

HAIRY COMB
Polynesians decorated their combs with braided human hair.

Polynesian dagger

The Silk Road

A camel train

NOT ALL EXPLORATION took place over rolling seas. The Silk Road, one of the oldest and most important land routes, was forged around 500 B.C., and was used until sea routes to China were opened up in about 1650. Along this road trade was conducted between China and Europe. Chinese merchants sent silk and spices westward to Europe over the fearsome mountains and deserts of Asia, while gold, silver, and horses were imported to China. However, nobody traveled the entire length of the Silk Road until Marco Polo in the 13th century. The road was about 4,300 miles (7,000 km) long and very dangerous, and nobody knew for certain what was at the other end. It passed through numerous kingdoms where each ruler demanded money or gifts from travelers. In addition, bandits would often pillage a traveling camel train. Because of these dangers, silk was passed from one merchant to another, with no trader traveling for more than a few hundred miles at a time! The Silk Road declined in importance after European ships began a regular trade with China around the southern tip of Africa.

PURCHASING POWER
Chinese silk and porcelain were very popular in Europe. These Spanish silver coins were sent to China in exchange for Chinese goods. On many of them you can see marks where Chinese merchants cut into them to make sure that they were solid silver!

Check marks

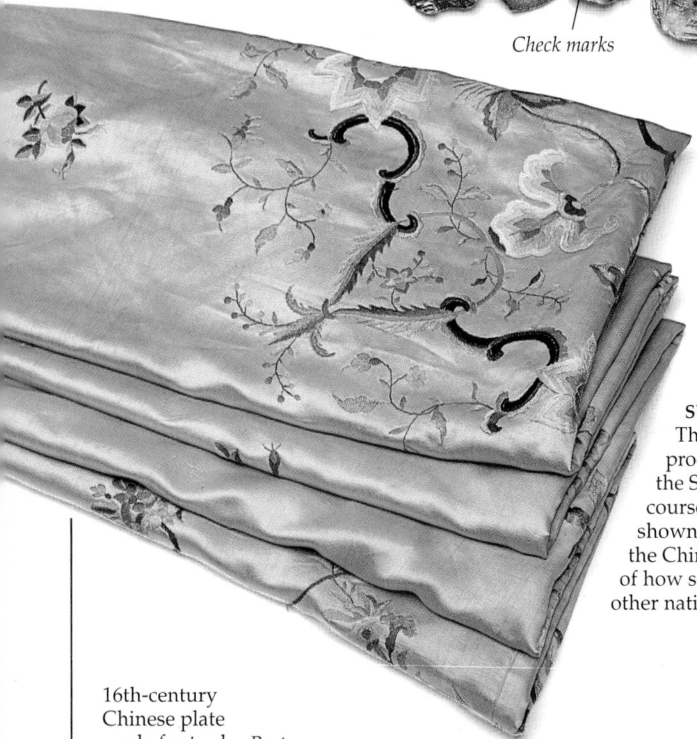

SUMPTUOUS SILK
The most important product traded along the Silk Road was, of course, silk – like this shown here. For centuries the Chinese kept the secret of how silk was made from other nations.

Turkish silver mount on rim

Dragon handles

14th-century Yuan dynasty jar

16th-century Chinese plate made for trade with Portugal

Portuguese ship motif

ORIENTAL PORCELAIN
Porcelain is a very hard translucent (lets light through) pottery invented by the Chinese. It was too fragile to transport in bulk along the Silk Road, but some small pieces were traded since it was much in demand. It was not until the sea routes opened up in the 17th century that trade in porcelain began in earnest.

14th- to 15th-century Ming dynasty bowl found in Kenya

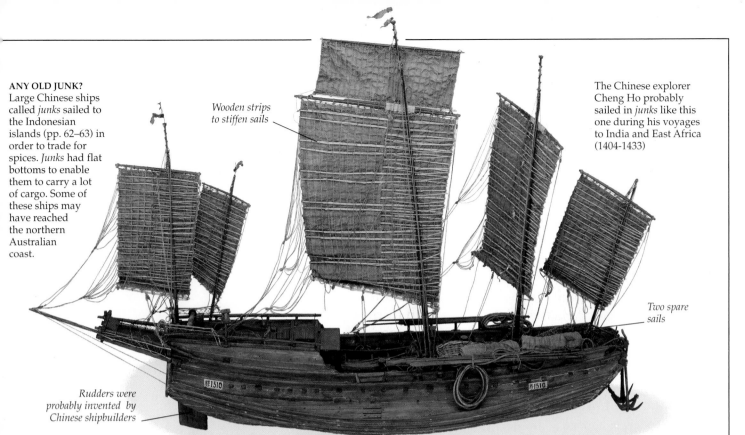

ANY OLD JUNK?
Large Chinese ships called *junks* sailed to the Indonesian islands (pp. 62–63) in order to trade for spices. *Junks* had flat bottoms to enable them to carry a lot of cargo. Some of these ships may have reached the northern Australian coast.

Wooden strips to stiffen sails

The Chinese explorer Cheng Ho probably sailed in *junks* like this one during his voyages to India and East Africa (1404-1433)

Two spare sails

Rudders were probably invented by Chinese shipbuilders

THE RUSSIAN OFFICER
Nicolay Przhevalsky was a Russian army officer who grew bored with soldiering and became an explorer instead. In 1867, he led a military expedition to explore vast areas of Central Asia. He later led four expeditions into unknown regions of Central Asia where he discovered kingdoms and countries previously unknown to Europeans.

This detail from a 17th-century Dutch map shows merchants in the East

TREACHEROUS ROUTE
This map shows the Silk Road and route of Marco Polo (see below). He used the Silk Road to cross Asia; it took him four years. He braved bandits, disease, and desert before returning by sea to Persia and then to Venice. He wrote an account of his travels, which many Europeans thought too fabulous to be true!

The Silk Road
Marco Polo's route

Venice
EUROPE   RUSSIA
Constantinople (Istanbul)
TURKEY
Tabriz
Maragheh   ASIA   Shachow   Shang-tu   Ning-hsia   Ta-tu
Acre Sultaniyeh   Kashgar
Herat   Balkh   CHINA   Feng-yuan
Kerman   HINDU KUSH   Chengtu
Hormuz   HIMALAYAS
Delhi   Tagaung
INDIAN   INDIA   BAY OF   SPICE
OCEAN   BENGAL   ISLANDS

MARCO POLO
In 1271, a Venetian merchant named Marco Polo traveled to China along the Silk Road with his father and uncle who had already visited the Chinese emperor Kublai Khan. Marco spent several years in China working as a government official before returning to Venice. This picture shows the Polos arriving at the Moslem city of Hormuz in the Persian Gulf.

THE ARTISTIC EXPLORER
Wherever Swedish explorer Sven Hedin traveled, he sketched and painted what he saw. Between 1890 and 1934, Hedin made several journeys into Central Asia, exploring and mapping new regions. He was twice held prisoner by bandits, and once nearly died of thirst.

OOST INDIEN.

Arab adventurers

Arab warriors traveled vast distances to conquer an empire that stretched from northern Spain across North Africa to northwest India in the sixth and seventh centuries. These holy wars were launched to spread the Islamic faith, and many Muslim communities were established. Arab merchants also pushed out in all directions to find new trading areas. Some Arab traders traveled across the Sahara on camels and penetrated central Asia on horseback. By the 13th century, Arabs were using *dhows* to sail across the Indian Ocean to purchase silks, spices, and jewels from India, Indonesia, and China. Other ships sailed down the East African coast to collect slaves (pp. 46–47), ivory, and gold.

An Arab street trader

SLAVE TRADE
Much of the Arab wealth came from slave trading. Some prisoners were captured in Europe and Asia, but most came from Africa. They were captured in battles or bought from local tribesmen, and then taken back to North Africa where they were sold to noblemen or craftsmen.

MARCHING CHAINS
The Arab slave trade continued up until the late 19th century when European powers took over most of Africa (pp. 46–47). The slaves captured inland were locked in chains during the long marches to the coast.

ARABIC QUADRANT
The quadrant, a quarter circle with a plumb line attached, was one of the earliest navigational instruments invented by Arabs.

Approximate latitude was calculated by lining up one straight side with a heavenly body and reading the position of the plumb line

Quadrant was made of wood or brass

EVER-LASTING DHOWS
Dhows have been used for centuries by Moslem traders in the Persian Gulf and Indian Ocean and are still in use today. They have triangular lateen sails rigged on one or two masts and are able to sail very close to the wind. They can also be handled by a small crew. Most of the early Arab voyages of exploration or trade were made in *dhows*.

18

David Livingstone (pp. 46–47) brought these Arab slave chains back from one of his African journeys

Ibn Batuta is attacked by pirates

BEWARE PIRATES!
Ibn Battuta was a great Arab traveler who, using known trade routes, traveled to almost every place in the Muslim world, writing about his adventures. All in all, he is thought to have traveled around 120,000 miles (193,000 km).

ARABIAN NIGHTS
Sinbad the Sailor was a favorite hero in Arabian adventure stories, many of which were based on true voyages. The Old Man of the Sea was a wicked magician who attempted to enslave sailors, but he was, of course, defeated by Sinbad.

TIMBUKTU
Located just south of the Sahara Desert, Timbuktu was an important town. Merchants visited the city to trade salt and trinkets for gold, ivory, and slaves. Some travelers used Timbuktu as a base from which to explore inland Africa.

The Age of Exploration

IT WAS IN EARLY 15TH-CENTURY PORTUGAL that the first great voyages of the "Age of Exploration" began. In 1415, Prince Henry of Portugal – known as Henry the Navigator – was given command of the port of Ceuta (N. Morocco) and its ships. He used these ships to explore the west coast of Africa, and he paid for numerous expeditions that eventually reached Sierra Leone on Africa's northwest coast. Later kings of Portugal financed expeditions that rounded the Cape of Good Hope on the southern tip of Africa, thus opening up trade routes to India, China, and the Indonesian and Philippine islands – "the Spice Islands." Portugal became immensely rich and powerful through its control of trade in this area.

Crow's nest

Bowsprit

Large hold for carrying cargo

PRINCE HENRY
Henry the Navigator sailed on only two voyages himself. However, up until 1460 he financed many voyages of exploration and founded a Portuguese school of navigation.

PASSAGE TO INDIA
Vasco da Gama's route took him via the Cape of Good Hope. He then sailed north along the east coast of Africa until he reached Malindi. There he took on board an Arab navigator who showed da Gama how to use the monsoon winds to cross the Indian Ocean – and reach India.

VASCO DA GAMA
Famous as the first European to sail to India, Vasco da Gama made his historic voyage around the Cape of Good Hope in 1497, and arrived in India in 1498. Two years later, a trading station established in India by the Portuguese was destroyed by local Moslems. Da Gama led a fleet of warships to exact revenge, and in 1502 his fleet destroyed the town of Calicut. In 1524, da Gama was appointed Portuguese viceroy of India, but he died almost as soon as he arrived there.

This statue of the angel San Raphael accompanied Vasco da Gama on his trip to India

AFRICAN IVORY

Once sea routes from Portugal to Africa had been opened up, Portuguese traders flocked to West Africa to collect ivory. This ivory statue was made by a West African craftsman in the 17th century and shows a Portuguese sailor in a crow's nest.

PORTUGUESE ENTERPRISE

In 1469, the Portuguese king granted Fernao Gomes trading rights with West Africa – on condition that he explore 350 miles (500 km) of coast each year. This map shows the coastline he had discovered by 1475.

TIN COIN

By the end of the 16th century, Portugal's considerable trading interests led to the formation of a large Portuguese empire in the East. This Portuguese coin was minted in Malaya (now Malaysia) in 1511.

THE FAVORITE SHIP

Most early Portuguese explorers made their voyages in small wooden sailing ships called *caravels*. These sturdy ships were able to withstand storms and had large holds for carrying cargo. Their lateen (triangular) sails enabled them to take advantage of a wind blowing from the side of the ship.

AZIMUTH COMPASS

This beautifully decorated Portuguese marine compass was made in 1780, but it incorporates the design of much earlier compasses.

MARK OF THE CROSS

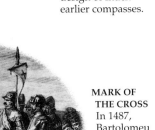

In 1487, Bartolomeu Dias became the first European to make a confirmed passage around the Cape of Good Hope. Before leaving, he erected a cross on the Cape to mark his discovery.

The New World

EVEN THE MOST EDUCATED Europeans knew little about the world outside Europe in 1480. South of the Sahara desert in North Africa stretched vast, impenetrable jungles. Asia was rarely visited, and the stories that travelers brought back were so amazing that not many people believed them (pp. 16–17). To the west lay the vast Atlantic Ocean, but nobody knew how wide the Atlantic was, nor what lay on the other side. Then, in 1480, the Italian navigator Christopher Columbus announced he had calculated that the East Indies lay only 2,795 miles (4,500 km) to the west. Few believed him, and indeed he was later proved wrong. Nevertheless, the Spanish king and queen paid for his expedition, and Columbus discovered America where he thought the East Indies should be. This voyage was one of the most important that took place during the Age of Exploration (pp. 20–21).

THE FIRST SEA ATLAS
In 1582, the Dutchman Lucas Wagenaer published a book containing detailed information about the coasts of western Europe. The frontispiece (above) was beautifully decorated with ships and nautical instruments.

SIR WALTER RALEIGH
During the late 16th century, Sir Walter Raleigh tried unsuccessfully to establish English colonies in "the New World" that Columbus had found. However, he is usually remembered more for the potatoes and tobacco plants that his captains returned with!

HANGING BEDS
When Columbus and his men reached the West Indies, they found the natives sleeping in hanging beds called "hamacas." The sailors copied this idea to make dry, rat-free beds above the dirty, wet decks. We now call these beds "hammocks."

SWEET FRUITS
The New World discovered by Columbus was inhabited by peoples who grew crops very different from those in Europe. These included pineapples and sweet potatoes, which were taken back to Europe.

REWARDS OF SUCCESS
When Christopher Columbus returned from his first voyage, he brought back strange people and objects from the New World to present to Ferdinand and Isabella. The king and queen were so impressed that they made Columbus an admiral and a nobleman.

Royal flag of Spain

AMERIGO'S LAND
America gets its name from "Amerigo's land," which was used on a map made in 1507 by Martin Waldseemuller. The map-maker named the land after Italian navigator Amerigo Vespucci, having read accounts of Vespucci's voyages to "the New World" and not realizing that Columbus had gotten there first.

SETTING A COURSE
Columbus took an astrolabe similar to this on his voyage of discovery, but preferred to work out his position at sea by "dead reckoning" – keeping records of his ship's speed and direction.

THE *SANTA MARIA*
The flagship of Columbus's voyage was the *Santa María*, a caravel from northern Spain. Like the other two ships of the expedition, the *Niña* and the *Pinta*, it was short and stocky with three masts. Columbus traveled on the *Santa María*, but when it was wrecked off the West Indies, he transferred to the *Niña* for the voyage home.

NEW WORLD MAP
Columbus made four voyages to the New World. Most of his time was spent exploring the West Indies, but on his third voyage, he reached the mainland near Panama, Central America.

NEW WORLD GOLD
In return for financing the expedition, Columbus promised to bring back gold for King Ferdinand and Queen Isabella of Spain. However, little gold was discovered until Cortés reached the Aztec Empire in 1519.

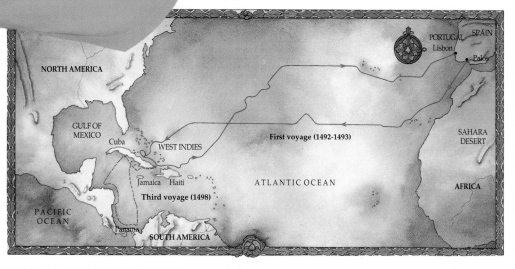

NORTH AMERICA

PORTUGAL
Lisbon
SPAIN
Palos

GULF OF MEXICO

Cuba

WEST INDIES

First voyage (1492-1493)

SAHARA DESERT

Jamaica Haiti

ATLANTIC OCEAN

AFRICA

Third voyage (1498)

PACIFIC OCEAN

Panama

SOUTH AMERICA

Around the world

ALTHOUGH FERDINAND MAGELLAN is credited with having made the first voyage around the world, he did not actually complete the journey himself. Of the five ships that made up his fleet, only one, the *Victoria*, returned after a grueling three-year journey, and Magellan was not on board. Ferdinand Magellan was a Portuguese gentleman who, like Christopher Columbus before him (pp. 22–23), thought he could navigate a westward route to the Spice Islands of the East. By 1500, Portugal had established a sea route to the Spice Islands around the Cape of Good Hope (pp. 62–63). Spain was eager to join in the highly profitable trade Portugal enjoyed with these islands, and in 1519, the king commissioned Magellan to forge his westward route. Magellan's journey took him through the dangerous, stormy passage at the tip of South America, now called the Strait of Magellan. Upon emerging into the calm ocean on the other side, Magellan referred to it as "the sea of peace," or Pacific Ocean. He was the first European to sail from the Atlantic Ocean to the Pacific Ocean.

MONSTER AHOY!
Sailors of Magellan's time were terrified of huge serpentine beasts they believed capable of eating men and sinking ships.

Antonio Pigafetta's 16th-century manuscript showing Magellan's journey

FERDINAND MAGELLAN
Ferdinand Magellan was a Portuguese adventurer of noble parentage. In 1518, he persuaded Charles I of Spain that he could reach the Spice Islands in the East by sailing around Cape Horn, and across the Pacific Ocean. He succeeded in reaching the islands, but became involved in a local war on one of them and was killed in battle.

CIRCLING THE EARTH
Battista Agnese's map was drawn after the return of the *Victoria*. Magellan's route through the Strait of Magellan is shown, but the extent of land to the south remains unclear. The approximate size of the Pacific Ocean is indicated, though Australia and most of the Pacific islands are missing.

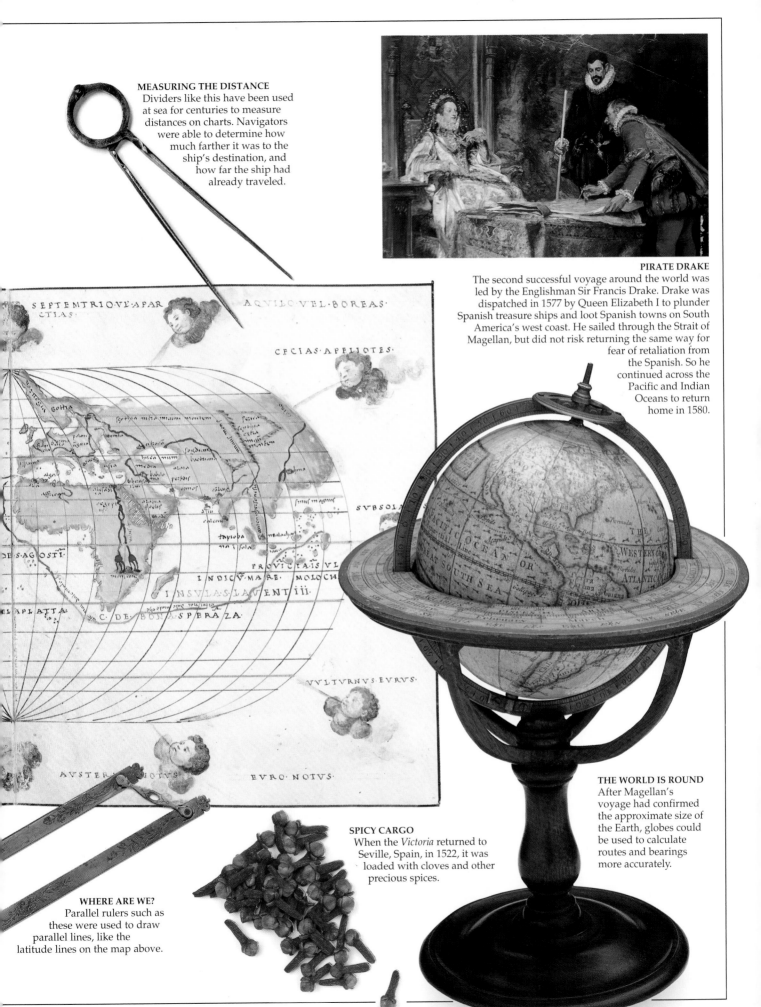

MEASURING THE DISTANCE
Dividers like this have been used at sea for centuries to measure distances on charts. Navigators were able to determine how much farther it was to the ship's destination, and how far the ship had already traveled.

PIRATE DRAKE
The second successful voyage around the world was led by the Englishman Sir Francis Drake. Drake was dispatched in 1577 by Queen Elizabeth I to plunder Spanish treasure ships and loot Spanish towns on South America's west coast. He sailed through the Strait of Magellan, but did not risk returning the same way for fear of retaliation from the Spanish. So he continued across the Pacific and Indian Oceans to return home in 1580.

THE WORLD IS ROUND
After Magellan's voyage had confirmed the approximate size of the Earth, globes could be used to calculate routes and bearings more accurately.

SPICY CARGO
When the *Victoria* returned to Seville, Spain, in 1522, it was loaded with cloves and other precious spices.

WHERE ARE WE?
Parallel rulers such as these were used to draw parallel lines, like the latitude lines on the map above.

Life at sea

Sailors in rigging

BEFORE THE INTRODUCTION of modern luxuries, life on board ship was hard for the ordinary sailor. Long voyages often meant being at sea for months – even years. Fresh food was unavailable, and even drinking water could be scarce. Terrible diseases – particularly scurvy (vitamin deficiency) – were common, resulting in many deaths at sea. The sailor's numerous duties included climbing the high masts and rigging to work the sails (often in the most hazardous weather conditions), taking turns on watch, and swabbing down filthy decks at regular intervals. Seamen spent what time they did have to themselves on hobbies or games, or on playing pranks on fellow crew members. Life on board ship changed little between 1500 and 1850. After this, the introduction of steam power and more sophisticated navigational aids made the sailor's life much more bearable.

PASSING THE TIME
Seamen on whaling ships often passed their spare time engraving designs on whales' teeth. The engraving was sometimes rubbed with black ink or soot to produce a clear image. This art is known as "scrimshaw."

SAILOR'S SEA CHEST
Sailors stored all their belongings in a sea chest, which took up little room on board. These chests had to be strong, as they had a variety of uses; they were sometimes used as seats, tables, and even beds. This chest has the name and date of its owner painted on it and is full of the kind of objects it might have originally held.

GOLD HOOPS
Sailors sometimes wore earrings. This gold pair belonged to a 19th-century American sailor named Richard Ward.

SEA BED
The hammock was adapted from a hanging bed Columbus discovered (pp. 22–23). Because the hammock swings from side to side, its occupant did not fall out in heavy seas.

Sailor's hat

18th-century log slate

Pencil for slate

Twist of tobacco

Penknife

Sailmaker's bag

Fid for splicing ropes

Seam rubber for flattening seams

Palm to protect hand

Needles and case

TOOLS OF THE TRADE
Few skills were more essential than that of the sailmaker. This bag contains the tools necessary for mending sails, repairing ropes, and sewing canvas.

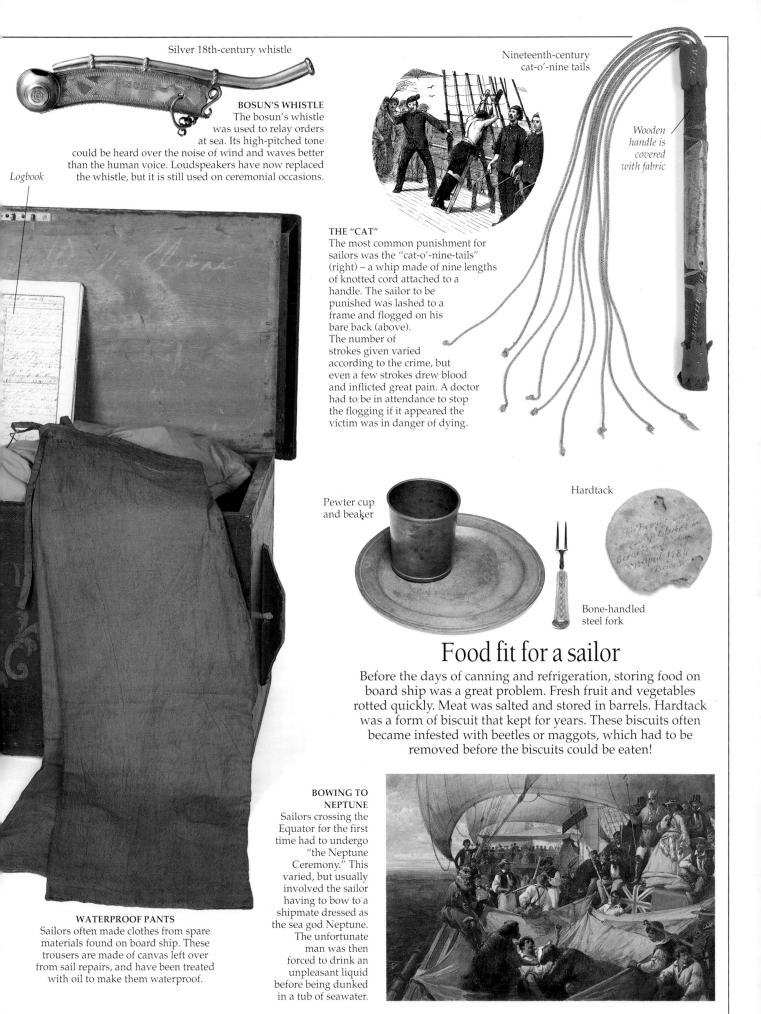

Silver 18th-century whistle

BOSUN'S WHISTLE
The bosun's whistle was used to relay orders at sea. Its high-pitched tone could be heard over the noise of wind and waves better than the human voice. Loudspeakers have now replaced the whistle, but it is still used on ceremonial occasions.

Nineteenth-century cat-o'-nine tails

Wooden handle is covered with fabric

Logbook

THE "CAT"
The most common punishment for sailors was the "cat-o'-nine-tails" (right) – a whip made of nine lengths of knotted cord attached to a handle. The sailor to be punished was lashed to a frame and flogged on his bare back (above). The number of strokes given varied according to the crime, but even a few strokes drew blood and inflicted great pain. A doctor had to be in attendance to stop the flogging if it appeared the victim was in danger of dying.

Pewter cup and beaker

Hardtack

Bone-handled steel fork

Food fit for a sailor

Before the days of canning and refrigeration, storing food on board ship was a great problem. Fresh fruit and vegetables rotted quickly. Meat was salted and stored in barrels. Hardtack was a form of biscuit that kept for years. These biscuits often became infested with beetles or maggots, which had to be removed before the biscuits could be eaten!

BOWING TO NEPTUNE
Sailors crossing the Equator for the first time had to undergo "the Neptune Ceremony." This varied, but usually involved the sailor having to bow to a shipmate dressed as the sea god Neptune. The unfortunate man was then forced to drink an unpleasant liquid before being dunked in a tub of seawater.

WATERPROOF PANTS
Sailors often made clothes from spare materials found on board ship. These trousers are made of canvas left over from sail repairs, and have been treated with oil to make them waterproof.

Tricks of the trade

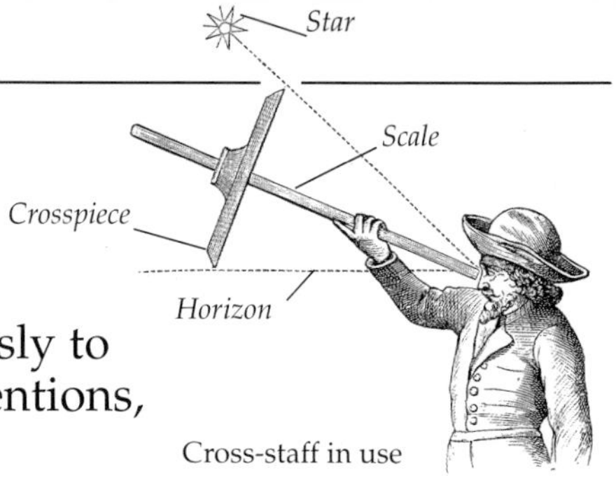

Star
Scale
Crosspiece
Horizon
Cross-staff in use

MODERN NAVIGATORS USE RADAR, radio, and satellites continuously to update the positions of their ships as they move. Before these inventions, navigation involved careful manual calculation. Navigators used instruments designed for observing the heavens, and related what they saw to a sea chart. They then took a reasonably short but safe course between two defined points, taking into account wind direction, currents, and rocks. Until nautical almanacs and marine chronometers were introduced in the 1760s, it was virtually impossible to find a ship's longitude. Navigators had to rely on estimates of their course and speed to guess their longtitude (that is, "dead reckoning"), and observations of the sun or the Pole (North) Star to work out their latitude (a useful corrective to dead reckoning).

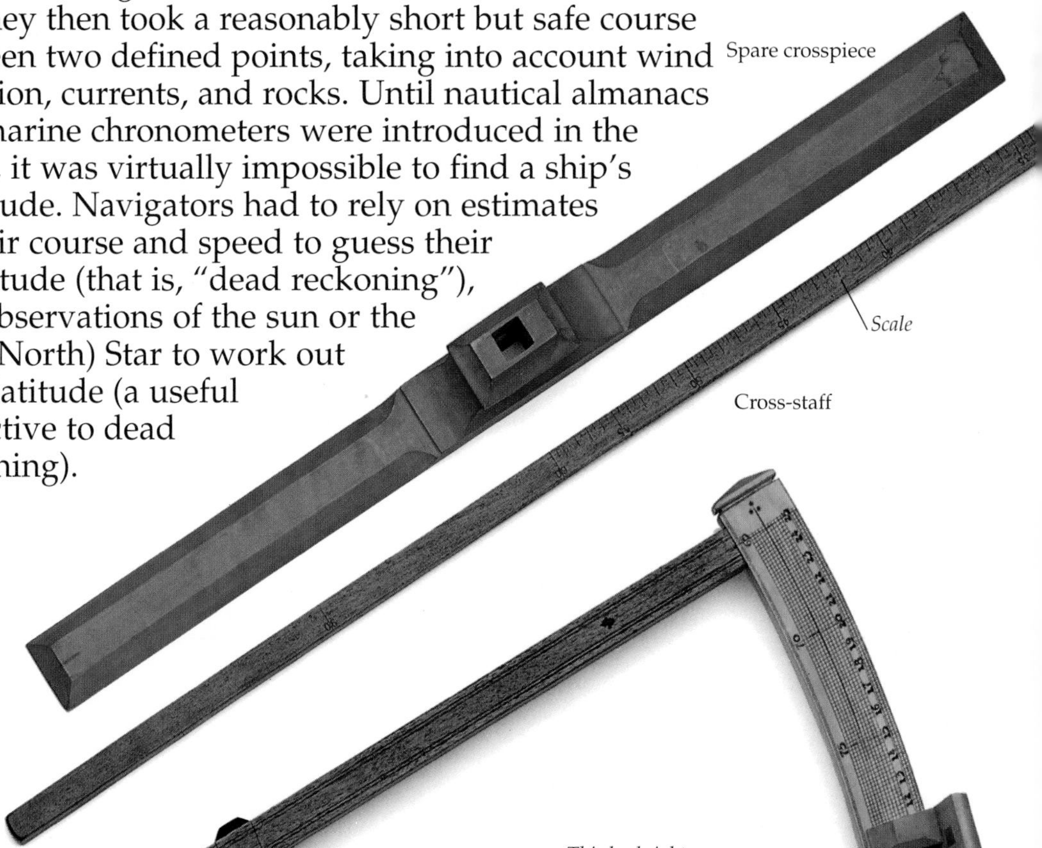

Spare crosspiece

Scale

Cross-staff

LODESTONE
Before the invention of the compass, lodestone (naturally magnetic iron oxide) was used to determine direction. When suspended, lodestone always points north. About 2,000 years ago, the Chinese discovered that if they stroked a soft iron rod with lodestone, it too would point north.

Peg

This backsight was positioned at the estimated latitude. This value was added to the reading on the peg to give the true latitude

Vane

Horizon slit

BACK STAFF
The back staff gave a ship's latitude (position north or south of the equator) by sighting on the sun, which was too bright to gaze at long enough to use the cross-staff. The navigator stood with his back to the sun, then lined up the backsight and the vane with the horizon. The peg on the smaller arc was moved until the shadow of the peg fell on the horizon slit. The combined angles of the backsight and peg gave the angle of the sun and hence the latitude of the ship.

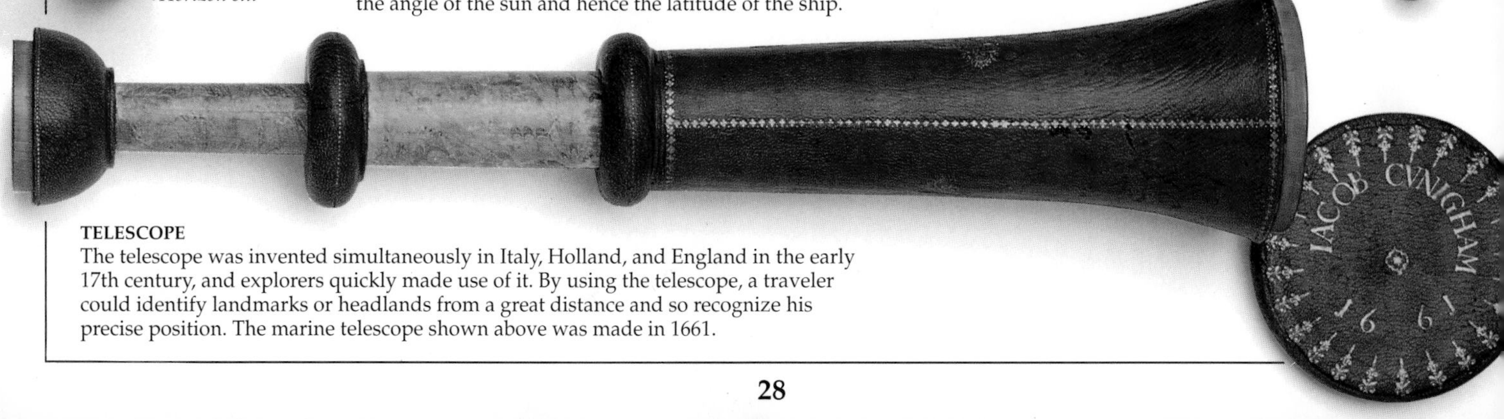

TELESCOPE
The telescope was invented simultaneously in Italy, Holland, and England in the early 17th century, and explorers quickly made use of it. By using the telescope, a traveler could identify landmarks or headlands from a great distance and so recognize his precise position. The marine telescope shown above was made in 1661.

CROSS-STAFF

The cross-staff was used from the late 15th century onward to determine a ship's latitude. Navigators knew that the observed angle between the horizon and the North Star changed, depending on the latitude of the ship. By placing one end of the cross-staff against the eye, the navigator could slide the crosspiece until one end lined up with the horizon and the other with the star. A scale on the stick gave the angle.

Crosspiece

Astrolabe in use

Mirror

Mirror

SEXTANT

The sextant was invented in the mid-18th century by the British Navy to replace the back staff and cross-staff. Using an arrangement of mirrors, the sextant can measure latitude to an accuracy of 0.01 of a degree. The navigator moves the index bar until the mirrors appear to line up the sun with the horizon. By reading the angle of the index bar, the angle of the sun (and therefore the ship's latitude) can be calculated.

Index bar

Sextant in use

Sextant that Captain Cook used on his third voyage to the Pacific (pp. 34 – 35)

MOORISH ASTROLABE

The astrolabe was an early instrument designed to determine latitude and was first used around 1300 by the Arabs. The astrolabe was suspended by a ring, and the navigator moved the alidade, or central rod, until it lined up with the North Star or the sun. The astrolabe was very inaccurate because it swung about on a moving ship.

COMPASS *below*

From the 12th century, magnetic compasses were used by seafaring explorers to define their courses and to determine in which direction to steer. Early compasses were magnetized needles that pointed north when suspended on string. Later, the needle was balanced on a central pivot and a card showing compass directions was mounted on top (as shown in the example below).

SHIP'S LOGBOOK

All ship's captains keep a logbook. Each day the captain records how far the ship has traveled and in which direction. The captain will also mention any events that occur, such as other ships sighted, landmarks passed, or sickness among the crew.

This log, dated 1770, was beautifully kept with pictures of passing ships and headlands

Gold and the gospel

W HEN COLUMBUS SET SAIL across the Atlantic (pp. 22–23), he hoped to discover a new trade route to China and the Spice Islands. Instead he found the West Indies – islands inhabited by tribes with a relatively primitive culture. These Indians had a few gold trinkets, but not much else of value. In the hope of establishing a trading colony on the mainland, Spain sent Hernando Cortés to Veracruz, Mexico, in 1519. Cortés was astonished to be met by richly dressed "ambassadors" who gave him valuable gifts of gold. Not content with these, however, Cortés resolved to travel inland in search of even greater riches. He found these riches when he reached the mighty Aztec Empire, which he and his troops totally destroyed in little more than two years. A similar fate awaited the equally wealthy Inca Empire of Peru, South America, which another Spaniard – Francisco Pizarro – conquered in 1532. Consumed with the greed for gold, many Spaniards arrived in South America. These "conquistadors" (conquerors) explored large areas and established several Spanish colonies.

Aztec gold figure

Aztec warriors earned the right to wear animal costumes by taking many prisoners

UNDER SIEGE
During one of the battles between the Spanish and Aztecs, Cortés' deputy, Pedro de Alvarado, and his men attacked a sacred meeting and were at once besieged by furious Aztec warriors. The Spaniards were rescued by Cortés, but not before they had lost many men.

DRINKING GOLD
In this illustration, some Indians are depicted pouring molten gold down the throats of captured soldiers out of revenge for the brutal treatment they have suffered at the hands of the gold-seeking Spaniards.

HARD HAT
Armor, such as this morion helmet, gave the Spanish soldiers an advantage in hand-to-hand combat. Apart from the obvious protection it gives the head, the upturned peak allows the wearer a good all-around view. Such helmets were usually worn by musketeers, who needed to be able to take careful aim when firing their guns.

BANG, BANG!
This matchlock gun is typical of weapons used by the conquistadors. The lack of carving and decoration shows that it was mass-produced for the army. Such a gun was accurate to about 160 ft (50 m).

LOOP THE LOOP

The snake was a powerful religious symbol in Mexico, and many snake-shaped ornaments, like this turquoise mosaic one, were made. Many Aztec temples were decorated with carved serpents; the entrance to one was a doorway in the shape of an open snake's mouth. People bitten by snakes were thought to be favored by the gods. The greatest snake god was Quetzalcóatl, the feathered serpent.

Mayan painted vase with lid

Warriors wearing animal costumes

PAINTED VASE

The Mayan civilization flourished in the rainforests of central America and Mexico, where the Mayan people built great stone cities and temples. The Mayans were also skilled potters. This advanced culture was at its height between 800 and 900, but survived until it was conquered by the Spanish in the 16th and 17th centuries.

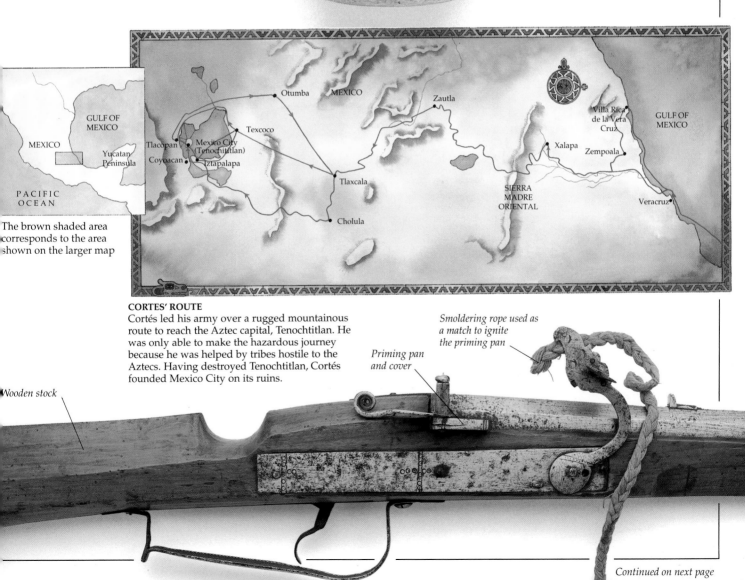

The brown shaded area corresponds to the area shown on the larger map

CORTÉS' ROUTE

Cortés led his army over a rugged mountainous route to reach the Aztec capital, Tenochtitlan. He was only able to make the hazardous journey because he was helped by tribes hostile to the Aztecs. Having destroyed Tenochtitlan, Cortés founded Mexico City on its ruins.

Wooden stock

Priming pan and cover

Smoldering rope used as a match to ignite the priming pan

Continued on next page

Continued from previous page

GOLD DOUBLOONS
Mexico and Peru were enormously rich in gold and silver. Much of the gold mined by the Spanish in South America was made into gold coins which were shipped back to Spain.

18th-century gold doubloons

Lion and castle, symbols of the Spanish crown

Pillars of Hercules, symbol of the Spanish Empire

A Spanish conquistador – maybe Pizarro himself – is depicted on the beaker

WOODEN BEAKER
This wooden beaker was made by an Inca craftsman in the mid-16th century. It was sent back to Spain after Pizarro's murder in 1541 by fellow Spanish soldiers in a personal feud. The Inca Empire was governed by Pizarro for eight years, during which time he imposed European administration and industry on the proud Inca Indians.

DEATH OF A KING
At his first meeting with the great Inca king, Atahualpa, Pizarro made a surprise attack and captured the king. Although Atahualpa paid a vast ransom, Pizarro could not risk freeing him and had him executed.

Quinoa shoot

Quinoa grain

"GRAIN OF THE GODS"
The food the Incas ate was plain and simple. Meals often consisted of roasted or boiled maize (corn), potatoes, and this grain called quinoa, also known as "grain of the gods."

TELL OR ELSE!
In 1539, Hernando de Soto landed in Florida and marched north in the never-ending Spanish search for gold. De Soto found no treasure, but was convinced that the local Indians were hiding their gold from him. He subjected them to incredibly cruel tortures in the hope that they would reveal where they had hidden the gold.

CRUEL RELIGION
The Aztec religion seems very cruel to us; several Aztec gods demanded blood sacrifices. Humans sacrificed to the war god Huitzilopochtli had their still-beating hearts cut out with a knife.

THE LAST CONQUISTADOR
In 1540, rumors of a rich city far to the north led to a large expedition led by Francisco Coronado. He marched through much of what is now the United States, discovering the Grand Canyon and almost reaching the Kansas River. However, Coronado found neither gold nor the fabled city.

Catholics use a string of beads called a rosary for counting prayers

The Gospel

The Catholic religion was of vital importance to the Spanish conquistadors. All Spanish expeditions were accompanied by a priest, who was expected both to conduct religious services and to convert to Christianity any "heathens" they encountered. Both priests and soldiers were disgusted by the religions they came across in the New World; human sacrifice was common, as was the worship of idols. The Spanish set about systematically destroying temples and executing local priests, which led to the total disruption of the Aztec and Inca societies. The policy was so widespread and complete that today the principal religion in Central and South America is Catholicism.

The Great South Sea

CAPTAIN JAMES COOK
This portrait of James Cook was painted after his return from his second voyage. His wife thought it was a good likeness, but considered his expression "a little too severe."

Aᴌᴍᴏꜱᴛ ᴀʟʟ ᴛʜᴇ ᴍʏꜱᴛᴇʀɪᴇꜱ surrounding the southern and central Pacific, "the Great South Sea," were solved during the late 18th century. Until then, Australia's east coast was unknown, and the two islands of New Zealand were thought to be one. However, in 1768, James Cook, an excellent navigator and cartographer (map drawer), set sail from Plymouth, England (pp. 36–37). One task given him by the Admiralty was to explore and chart the region. During this voyage, he charted the New Zealand coasts and Australia's east coast. His next voyage, in 1772, took him to Antarctica and many Pacific islands, and his third, in 1776, led to the discovery of the Hawaiian islands and exploration of the Alaskan coast.

Dividers

Penholder

Dividers

Parallel ruler

Sector

ABEL TASMAN
During the 17th century, the Dutchman Abel Tasman sailed around the southern coast of Australia – without seeing it – and discovered New Zealand and Fiji.

DRAWING TOOLS
These 18th-century instruments are the type Captain Cook would have used to draw up his extremely fine charts of the Pacific Ocean.

UNKNOWN LAND
This Dutch map of around 1590 shows a land labeled "Terra Australis Nondum Cognita," which means "Unknown Southern Land." Scientists argued over whether this southern land was one large land mass.

SEA TIME
An accurate timepiece was essential for determining a ship's longitude. This chronometer was used by Cook on his second voyage.

JUMPING DOG
Captain Cook and his men came across several animals completely unknown to Europeans. The peculiar kangaroo puzzled them. Cook wrote, "I should have taken it for a wild dog but for its running, in which it jumped like a hare."

DEATH OF COOK
Cook was always careful to maintain good relations with the native peoples he met. At first, the Hawaiians thought he was a god, but when one of Cook's men died, they realized he and his followers were mere mortals. The Hawaiians later stole a boat from Cook's ship, and when Cook went ashore to recover it, a scuffle broke out during which he was killed.

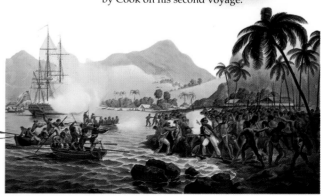

PORTABLE STOVE
Most meals on board ship were cooked in the galley, but the wealthy naturalist Sir Joseph Banks (pp. 50–51), who sailed on Cook's first voyage, prepared his own meals with this miniature stove.

SOLID SOUP
Cook was the first sea captain to take measures against scurvy (vitamin deficiency). When mixed with hot water, this solid soup of marrow stock made a nourishing broth and was thought to help prevent scurvy.

POLYNESIAN VILLAGE
This picture shows Nagaloa, a Fijian village, as it appeared to early travelers.

FEATHER GORGET
The Polynesian kings and chiefs Cook met dressed in elaborate clothes made from the feathers of local birds. Cook brought back this magnificent "gorget," or chest ornament, worn by Tahitian kings.

BREADFRUIT
The large white fruits of the breadfruit tree that grows wild in Polynesia ripen easily and are a good source of food.

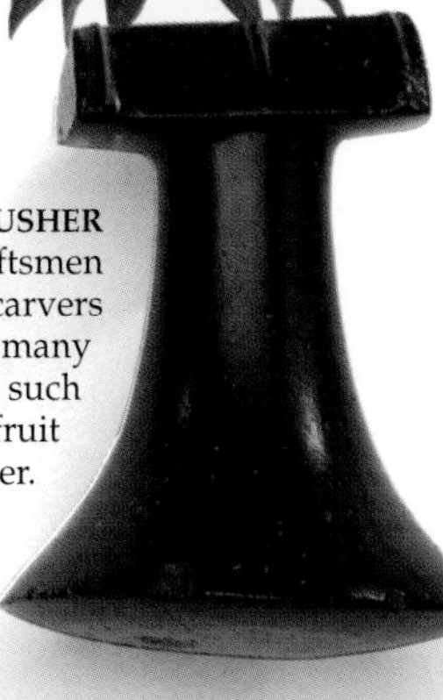

CARVED CRUSHER
Polynesian craftsmen were expert woodcarvers and produced many beautiful objects, such as this breadfruit pounder.

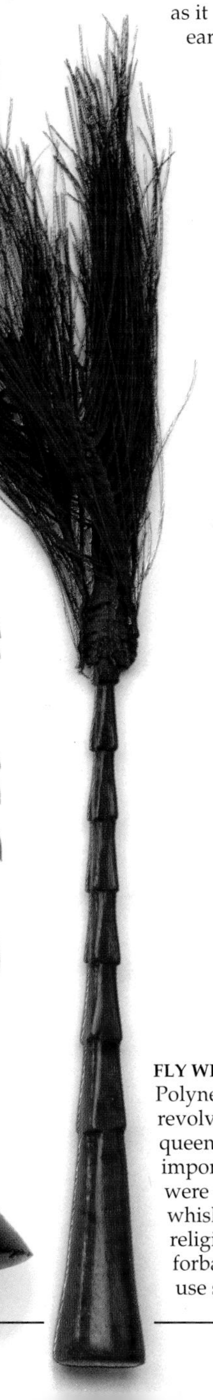

FLY WHISK
Polynesian society revolved around kings, queens, and nobles. Only important men and women were allowed to carry fly whisks like this. Strong religious rules called "taboos" forbade ordinary people to use such items.

The Endeavour

T<small>HE SHIP</small> C<small>OOK CHOSE</small> for his first voyage in 1768 (pp. 34–35) was the *Endeavour*, a rounded, tub-shaped coal-carrier. These coal-carriers were specially built to carry about 600 tons of coal from northern England to London. They had deep, broad waists, no figureheads, and narrow sterns. Cook had sailed in coal-carriers as a young man, so he had experience in handling these strongly built ships. He knew that if he needed to he could beach the *Endeavour* without causing it any damage.

The Crew

As a naval vessel on scientific duty, the *Endeavour* had a mixed crew. In addition to Cook, there were several other officers to help navigate the ship and to make decisions. The sailors were skilled carpenters, sailmakers, musicians, or other craftsmen. The marines were armed soldiers who enforced discipline on the ship and protected the ship from pirates or hostile natives. Scientists and artists also traveled on the *Endeavour*. They did not help with the running of the ship, but spent their time making observations, conducting experiments, and sketching new sights.

Mizzenmast

Mainmast

Spanker

James Cook and Joseph Banks in cabin

British naval flag

Coal

Planks of wood

1.
2.
3.
4.
5.
6.
7.
8.
9.
10.
11.
12.
13.

Foremast

Bowsprit

As a cat-collier, the *Endeavour* was
ship-rigged and capable of carrying a
heavy cargo and many men. Ship-
rigging meant that a ship had at least
three square-rigged masts. The square
sails were always turned to take the
wind on one side only. The mizzen
mast also carried a fore and aft sail
that could take the wind on either
side. This rig enabled the *Endeavour* to
sail well in most types of weather and
to survive the fiercest storms. The
cargo hold could carry 600 tons, and
was specially converted for the
voyage to contain stores and scientific
equipment. As the voyage continued,
the stores were used up and replaced
with plant and animal samples.

SOME OF COOK'S CREW
1. Matthew Cox and Archibald Wolfe, seamen; 2. John
Thompson, cook; 3. Herman Sporing, naturalist; 4.
Sydney Parkinson, artist; 5. Alexander Buchan, artist;
6. Thomas Simmonds, seaman; 7. John Reynolds,
servant; 8. William Monkhouse, surgeon; 9. Charles
Green, astronomer; 10. Dr. Daniel Solander, botanist;
11. John Ravenhill, sailmaker; 12. Antonio Ponto,
seaman; 13. Drummer and marines; 14. Thomas Jordan
and James Tunley, servants; 15. James Magra and
Richard Littleboy, seamen; 16. John Satterley and
George Novell, carpenter and carpenter's mate; 17.
Thomas Hardman, boatswain's mate; 18.
Thomas Knight, seaman; 19. John Gathrey,
boatswain; 20. Richard Pickersgill,
master's mate; 21. Alexander
Simpson, seaman; 22. John
Goodjohn, seaman; 23.
Joseph Childs, seaman;
24. Thomas Mathews,
servant; 25. John
Woodworth, seaman;
26. Richard Hughes,
seaman

14. 17. 18. 21. 23. 26.

24.

16. 19.

15. 20. 22. 25.

Barrels of rum
and water

Spare sails

Seamens'
chests

Hammocks

37

Across Australia

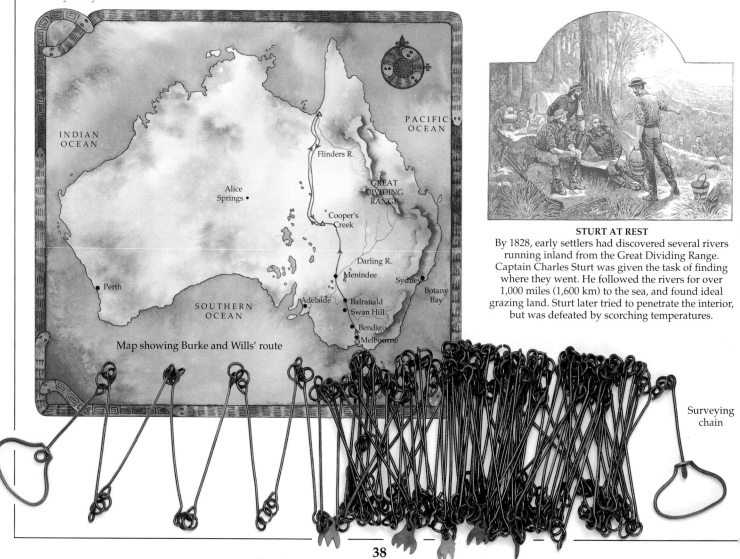

THE FIRST EUROPEAN to land in Australia was the Dutchman Dirk Hartog, who touched on the west coast in 1616. However, it was not until James Cook's voyage (pp. 34–35), and later those of Matthew Flinders, that Europeans gained a clear idea of the extent of this vast continent. The first settlers arrived in Botany Bay in 1788. For many years, settlers were restricted to the coast, as no route over the Blue Mountains west of Sydney could be found. Then, in 1813, John Blaxland, William Lawson, and William Wentworth tried the novel approach of climbing the mountain ridges instead of following the valleys, and they found a way over the mountains to the lush highlands. After this breakthrough, others attempted to penetrate the dry and lifeless interior beyond the highlands, but some died on their travels. This fate was narrowly escaped by Peter Warburton, a retired police commissioner, who in 1873 became the first man to cross the great deserts around Alice Springs.

"THE SEA!"
In 1862, John Stuart led a team north from Adelaide to find the northern coast. Suddenly, one of the men turned and shouted, "The sea!" Everyone was amazed. They thought their goal lay many miles ahead.

THE ULTIMATE PRICE
In 1860, Robert Burke and W. John Wills set out from Melbourne. Like Stuart, they too were attempting to cross Australia. Supplies and men were left at Cooper's Creek, and Burke, Wills, and two others rode on ahead. They found the sea, but Burke and Wills died on the return journey.

Map showing Burke and Wills' route

STURT AT REST
By 1828, early settlers had discovered several rivers running inland from the Great Dividing Range. Captain Charles Sturt was given the task of finding where they went. He followed the rivers for over 1,000 miles (1,600 km) to the sea, and found ideal grazing land. Sturt later tried to penetrate the interior, but was defeated by scorching temperatures.

Surveying chain

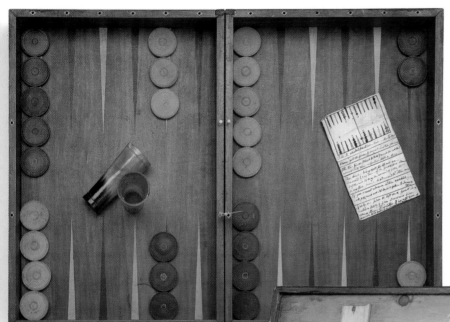

FLINDERS' FLUTE *above*
This flute belonged to Matthew Flinders (below). He may have played it during his long sea voyages.

MATTHEW FLINDERS
In 1798, Matthew Flinders, an English naval officer, was sent to explore Van Diemen's land (now Tasmania) – which he sailed right around. Three years later, he sailed around Australia, charting much of the coastline and proving that it was one continuous land mass.

PASSING THE TIME
Flinders had this backgammon set with him on his long voyage around the coast of Australia. It was the custom for naval captains on long voyages to invite the ship's officers to social evenings, when they would play games such as this. Flinders was also accompanied by his cat, Trim, until the unfortunate animal disappeared and was presumed dead on the French island of Mauritius in 1803.

BOX OF BELONGINGS
Flinders always made sure that his belongings fit into this wooden sea chest, which he took with him on his voyages. Space on board his ships was very limited, so he and his crew had to take as little as possible with them.

SURVEYING CHAIN
At the time Australia was being explored, surveying equipment was rather primitive. Land was measured in "chains"– each of which was 66 ft (20 m) long – like this one (left) that dates from Flinders' time. When explorers found a suitable place for a harbor or a settlement, they surveyed it carefully for future use.

The Northwest Passage

ONE OF THE GREATEST GOALS of maritime explorers was to find the fabled Northwest Passage, a route from Europe to China around the north of North America (pp. 62–63). The more obvious routes around the south of South America and Africa were blocked during the 16th century by Spanish and Portuguese warships (pp. 20–21, 24–25). Several mariners explored the frigid northern waters, but they were all defeated by the extreme cold and unfavorable winds. The search for the Northwest Passage was abandoned for a while, but in 1817, the British government offered £20,000 ($50,000) to whoever found the Passage. Many expeditions followed, the most tragic of which was that of Sir John Franklin in 1845, from which nobody returned. Eventually, in 1906, Norwegian sailor Roald Amundsen (pp. 54–55) steamed through the Northwest Passage after a three-year journey.

FROZEN SEAS
On Dutch navigator Willem Barents' third attempt to find a northerly route to China (1595–1597), ice pushed his ship out of the sea. His crew survived the winter, but Barents died on the return journey.

JOHN CABOT
In 1497, at the command of Henry VII, Italian-born John Cabot left Bristol in England to find a quick route to the Spice Islands off China's coast. He got as far as Newfoundland (pp. 62–63), which had already been discovered by the Vikings (pp. 12–13).

GIOVANNI DA VERRAZANO
In 1524, this Italian navigator found New York Bay and Narragansett Bay for the French. Here his boat is moored off what is now Newport, Rhode Island.

Handle made from two pieces of bone riveted to outer side of blade

Bone handle bound with leather and gut

SIR MARTIN FROBISHER
In 1576, Queen Elizabeth I of England dispatched Martin Frobisher to find the Northwest Passage to China. He failed to do this, but he did discover Baffin Island, the bay of which is named after him. He returned home with what he thought was rock containing gold, but it turned out to be iron pyrites, now known as "fool's gold."

Map showing Hudson's and Franklin's route

INUIT BONE KNIVES
These Inuit (northern Eskimo) knives, found by one of the search parties sent to look for Franklin, are evidence of the tragic fate of his expedition. Local Inuit made the knives with scraps of steel from Franklin's abandoned ships. They sharpened the steel to produce a cutting edge and attached it to handles made from bone.

BOWS AND ARROWS

These weapons were found being used by Inuit hunters ten years after Franklin's death. The arrowheads are made from supplies left by Franklin's expedition.

Iron head
Copper head
Iron head
Bone
Wooden shaft

Inuit in canoe

HENRY HUDSON

In 1609, Henry Hudson (who had already made two voyages north for England) was employed by the Dutch East India Company to search for a Northeast Passage. He made one attempt, then sailed west in search of the Northwest Passage. In 1610, he set out again and discovered Hudson Strait and Hudson Bay. In June 1611, his crew mutinied. Hudson and eight others were set adrift and never heard from again.

SNOW GOGGLES

Arctic sun shining on snow is dazzling and can cause temporary blindness. These leather goggles, which cut down the sun's glare, belonged to Sir John Franklin.

GOURMET FOOD

This tin of roast beef was found in 1958 near the last-known site of the Franklin Expedition and was almost certainly part of their supplies. Tins like this were sealed with lead, which is thought to have caused some health problems. On an earlier trip to the Arctic, Franklin and his men had been reduced to eating "pieces of singed hide mixed with lichen, and the horns and bones of a dead deer fried with some old shoes"!

ROAST BEEF.

LAST MESSAGE

In 1859, the 14-year mystery of Franklin's fate was solved when this message was found by Captain Francis McClintock, who was searching for signs of the expedition at the request of Lady Franklin. The message was written in April 1848 by Lieutenant Gore, one of the expedition members, and recorded the death of Franklin, together with details of the plan to march overland to safety. None of the men on the expedition completed the journey.

ICE–BOUND!

Sailing in frozen northern seas was fraught with danger, and ships frequently became stuck in ice. This was the fate of Franklin's two ships, the *Erebus* and *Terror*.

One of Franklin's ships, *Terror*, stuck in ice

North America tamed

WHILE CENTRAL AND SOUTH America were being explored by gold-hungry Spaniards (pp. 30–33), North America remained virtually unexplored. It was not until the late 16th and early 17th centuries that navigators such as Henry Hudson (pp. 40–41), Jacques Cartier, and Samuel de Champlain charted the eastern coast. English and French settlers followed, establishing towns along the East coast and along the St. Lawrence River. It was from these colonies that trappers and frontiersmen pushed inland. In 1803, the French emperor, Napoleon Bonaparte, sold Louisiana to the United States for just $15,000,000. One year later, President Thomas Jefferson sent Meriwether Lewis and William Clark to explore and chart this newly acquired region. Other journeys of exploration followed; gradually the vast interior of the United States was surveyed and mapped.

ARROWS AND GUNS
While Samuel de Champlain was exploring around the St. Lawrence River in 1609, he befriended the local Huron Indian tribe. De Champlain joined with them in a battle against the Iroquois. The Hurons won – their rivals were totally overcome by de Champlain's guns.

JACQUES CARTIER
In his search for the Northwest Passage, French navigator Jacques Cartier led three voyages to the east coast of North America. His greatest discovery was the St. Lawrence River in 1534. In 1535, Cartier pushed up river as far as Montreal in Canada, but could go no farther by water because of the rapids.

TRAVELLING LIGHT
Until the 18th century, the only way into the interior of North America was by river. Early explorers traveled in canoes made of birch bark stretched over a wooden frame. These canoes were light and easily controlled.

Cartier's route
Champlain's route
Lewis & Clarks's route
Frémont's route

ROCKY MOUNTAINS
GREAT PLAINS
PACIFIC OCEAN
Fort Clatsop
Fort Clark
Fort Mandan
Lake Superior
NEWFOUNDLAND
Quebec
Montreal
Lake Huron
Lake Ontario
Lake Michigan
Lake Erie
Missouri R.
Great Salt Lake
Kansas City
St. Louis
ATLANTIC OCEAN
SAN FRANCISCO BAY

This token was worth one beaver skin

N°3214 ONE SHILLING Sterlg 1845.
Hudsons Bay Company.
Promise to pay the Bearer on Demand
the Sum of ONE SHILLING for YORK FACTORY, in RUPERTS LAND
in a Bill of Exchange payable Sixty days after Sight at the
Hudsons Bay House, London. 3214
LONDON, the 1st day of May 1845. For the Governor & Company
of Adventurers of England Trading into Hudsons Bay.
N° 3214 A Barclay SECRETARY.
Issued at York Factory, the 4th day of March 1846 by
GOVERNOR.
Accountant.

Many beavers fell prey to
trappers, as their fur was much in
demand

RIVER ROUTES
French traders in search of furs acquired by
local Indian tribes established routes into
the interior along the Missouri River.
Sometimes they took their pets
with them!

*Pointed blade
with long
cutting edge*

BOWIE KNIFE
A good, heavy
hunting knife
was essential to
all settlers and
frontiersmen. The Bowie
knife – named after the
pioneer Jim Bowie – was one of
the best. The wide blade could inflict
deadly wounds and it was tough
enough to cope with heavy-duty
hunting work such as skinning.

TRADING MONEY
The Hudson's Bay Trading Company
issued its own money – notes like this
could be exchanged for English silver coins
at its headquarters in London. Brass tokens
were given to trappers and Indians in
exchange for beaver skins. These could
then be used to buy food and supplies
from the Company.

This scalp belonged
to an Indian from
the Eastern
Woodlands

Birchbark canoes like this
were used by the now-
extinct Beothuk Indian tribe
of Newfoundland

CLAIMING THE MISSISSIPPI
In April 1682, French trader and explorer Robert
Cavelier, Sieur de la Salle, stood at the mouth of
the mighty Mississippi River and claimed it for
France. He also claimed the
surrounding land, naming
it Louisiana in honor of
King Louis XIV.

HAIR-RAISING!
The Indian tribes
encountered by North
American explorers were often at war with
each other. The scalp of an enemy killed in
battle was one of their most important war trophies; the
successful warrior would remove the skin and hair from
the top of the victim's head. Sometimes they would then
mount the scalp onto a wooden frame.

Continued on next page

CHARLES WILKES
This wooden mask was presented to Charles Wilkes, a U.S. naval officer and explorer, when he visited and mapped the western coast of North America in about 1841. The mask was carved by Pacific northwest Indians. Wilkes also sailed south and charted the region of Antarctica that now bears his name – Wilkes Land.

RIVER RAPIDS
In 1789, Scottish explorer and trader Sir Alexander Mackenzie set out to explore north-west Canada. He was the first European to reach the Mackenzie River, which he followed to the Arctic Ocean.

PIKES PEAK
Zebulon Pike was famous for giving his name to Pikes Peak in Colorado, which he discovered in 1806, and his expedition charted large areas of the western plains and mountains.

Pencil

MEASURING TAPE
Nineteenth-century surveyors used linen measuring tapes like this one, which was stored in a leather case that also held a notebook and pencil.

PLANTING THE FLAG
John Frémont, a U.S. army officer, led several expeditions into the Far West. In 1842 he surveyed the Oregon Trail up the Platte River to South Pass. The following year, his second expedition took him over the Colorado Rockies, where he planted the flag on what he thought was the highest peak. In 1853, he searched unsuccessfully for a railroad route across the continent to California.

DETAILED DIARY

Lewis and Clark kept careful notes in the journal above of everything they found. They recorded geographical details of mountains and rivers, as well as information about the local Indian tribes and wildlife.

PAINTED PRIZE

This buffalo robe was collected by Meriwether Lewis and William Clark during their trek across America to the Pacific Ocean via the Missouri and Columbia rivers in 1804–1806. The robe is painted with a scene of Mandan and Minnetaree Indians fighting the Sioux and the Arikara.

WILLIAM CLARK

Clark was 33 years old when he co-commanded the first American expedition to explore territories between the Mississippi River and the Pacific Ocean. He was responsible for mapping the terrain and for maintaining discipline.

Clark's compass

MERIWETHER LEWIS

Both Lewis and Clark were soldiers, and although Lewis was younger, he was senior in rank. It was Lewis who organized the expedition and who recruited the men to take part.

WHERE THE BUFFALO ROAM

Early explorers of North America were amazed to see millions of buffalo roaming the plains. The herds were so vast that they sometimes stretched right across the horizon. This painting is by the great 19th-century naturalist John Audubon.

The unknown continent

FOR MANY CENTURIES, Africa was known as the Dark Continent by Europeans. While navigators were charting the oceans, and explorers traveled across the other continents, the African interior remained a blank on world maps – largely because it was such a dangerous place. Tropical diseases capable of killing a European within a day were common, and the jungles were full of lions, crocodiles, and African tribes that, threatened by the sudden "invasion" of strangers, could be aggressive and warlike. From about 1850, the Dark Continent became "brighter." Medicines to cure the most dangerous diseases were discovered, and modern guns could shoot animals and frighten tribal warriors. While some explorers followed the tropical rivers of central Africa to discover the great lakes – in particular, the Nile's source – others hiked the plains of southern Africa, or explored deep into the jungle as missionaries.

"DR. LIVINGSTONE, I PRESUME?"
So said journalist Henry Stanley when he met David Livingstone in the remote village of Ujiji in 1871 by Lake Tanganyika. Livingstone, a British physician and missionary who crossed Africa trying to abolish the Arab slave trade (pp. 18–19), had vanished in 1866.

JOHN HANNING SPEKE
Speke was an English explorer who made several journeys into central Africa. In 1858, he traveled with Burton to Lake Tanganyika, and then pushed on alone to discover Lake Victoria. In 1862, he went back to prove that the Nile flowed out of Lake Victoria.

AFRICAN WILDLIFE
Speke was also a naturalist. Wherever he went, he made notes and drawings of the wildlife and plants he saw. These sketches are of rhinoceroses.

SENSIBLE HEADGEAR
This was the hat Stanley was wearing when he met Dr. Livingstone. Many early travelers in Africa wore these hats to protect themselves from sunstroke.

WHITE RHINOCEROS.

White rhinos are now threatened with extinction

DRESSING THE PART
Sir Richard Burton was an English army officer who learned to speak Arabic and twenty-eight other languages. Dressed as an Arab, he traveled extensively through southern Asia and East Africa, where no European had been before. He also explored much of tropical Africa and parts of South America.

CONGO ARROWS
These lethal Pygmy arrows were shot into Livingstone's boat on his Zambezi River trip.

HAZARDOUS HIPPO
Like many explorers, Livingstone carried out much of his exploration by boat. He found it quicker and easier to travel by water than by land, but river travel could be dangerous. On one occasion, Livingstone's boat was overturned by a hippopotamus and much equipment was lost.

BATTERED BLUE CAP
Livingstone was wearing this cap when Stanley found him. Livingstone, who once said "the mere animal pleasure of traveling in a wild, unexplored country is very great," continued to explore lands around Lake Tanganyika, where he died of disease in 1873.

Livingstone's compass

Livingstone's magnifying glass

Livingstone's wooden quill pen

MONSTER MAP
By the time Descalier drew this 16th-century map, seamen had sailed around Africa. The map shows the coasts fairly accurately, but the interior is a blank filled in with imaginary features. Descalier had to guess the source of the Nile; its true source was not found until three hundred years later.

BANG, BANG!
This powerful elephant gun belonged to Sir Samuel Baker, who with his wife explored much of Africa looking for the Nile's source. Baker discovered Lake [Alb]ert in 1864 and was later [th]e governor of Sudan by the ruler of Egypt.

Naturalist explorers

An unusual way of collecting insects!

Aᴌᴛʜᴏᴜɢʜ ᴀᴅᴠᴇɴᴛᴜʀᴇ ᴀɴᴅ ᴩʀᴏꜰɪᴛ were the motives for many journeys of exploration, the thirst for scientific knowledge also became a powerful force in the late 18th and 19th centuries. It was a time when many naturalist explorers penetrated unknown territory with the specific purpose of discovering new species of animals, insects, and plants. Although earlier explorers had reported details of the strange and wonderful wildlife they had found, it was not until the late 18th century that naturalists began explorations with the sole aim of gathering scientific information. As well as greatly enhancing our knowledge of the world, these expeditions often brought great fame to those who were fortunate enough to discover new species.

HENRY BATES
Henry Bates, one of the greatest amateur naturalist explorers, studied natural history for several years before he accompanied Alfred Wallace (below right) to the Amazon rain forest in 1848. Bates spent 11 years searching for insects in areas never before visited by Europeans.

DETAILED STUDY
It was through this microscope that naturalist Charles Darwin studied insects and other small animals. What he saw helped him to form his theories of evolution.

SPECIMEN SHIP
In 1831, the British Royal Navy sent the ship *Beagle* (above) to explore the South Atlantic and South Pacific oceans. It was the custom to take a naturalist on such voyages, and 22-year-old Darwin was given the post. Darwin collected many specimens of insects and animals to study.

CREEPY-CRAWLIES
These are just a few of the beetles that Darwin collected on his journey.

Brass chloroform bottle

Ivory-handled pins

BOTTLE AND PINS
Insect collectors used chloroform to kill specimens quickly and painlessly. The insects were then pinned up for detailed study.

BANKS' BUTTERFLIES
Joseph Banks was a wealthy amateur naturalist. In 1768, he set sail with Captain Cook (pp. 34–35). Cook was under orders to explore the Pacific Ocean, and Banks went to study the animal and plant life. These butterflies were among the large collection of insects he brought back from Australia.

GENTLE PRISON
Naturalists used delicate nets like this to capture insects. These nets are so lightweight that they do not damage the delicate wings and legs in any way.

MARY KINGSLEY
Nineteenth-century Victorian England was a time when most respectable women stayed at home – but not Mary Kingsley! She left the comforts of her home to explore West Africa in search of new animals. Her determination was respected by the men of her time, and her work was highly acclaimed.

FISH FETISH
By Mary Kingsley's time, actual specimens were required to prove that new species really did exist. Mary was particularly interested in fish. She preserved this snoutfish in alcohol and carefully brought it back to Britain from the Ogowe River in Africa.

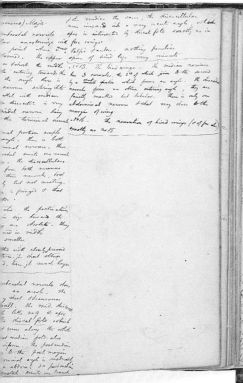

PERFECT PAGES
Henry Bates kept meticulous records of all the insect species he found. The pages of his notebooks, two of which are shown here, are full of beautifully colored illustrations and detailed written descriptions. During his years in South America, he discovered over 8,000 new insect species, 600 of which were butterflies.

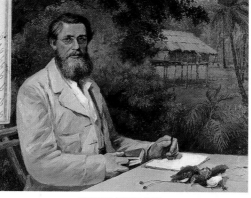

ALFRED WALLACE
Alfred Wallace traveled widely to discover new species that he hoped would prove the theories of his friend Charles Darwin. In 1848, he traveled to South America with Henry Bates, where he stayed for four years. In 1854, he left Britain for Indonesia and remained there for the next eight years collecting new insect species and exploring remote inland valleys.

Continued on next page

Plant collectors

The search for new plant species combines several of the most important ambitions of an explorer. By traveling to unknown regions in the hope of discovering new plants, the botanist (a person who studies plants) explorer combines the thrill of adventure with the excitement of scientific discovery. There is also money to be made from finding new plants, and many botanist explorers have become rich through their findings. However, the majority of 18th- and 19th-century botanist explorers were famous only in scientific circles. Today's naturalists campaign actively against the destruction of rain forests and the pollution of other habitats, and they are very much in the public eye.

VON HUMBOLDT AND BONPLAND
Alexander von Humboldt and Aimé Bonpland traveled throughout South America during the early 19th century studying geology and collecting plants. This painting shows them seated among their instruments and specimens in a jungle camp.

Shoot from a *cinchona* plant

Cinchona bark from which quinine is obtained

PRESSED PLANTS
These pressed eucalyptus leaves were brought back from Australia in the 19th century by Allan Cunningham. He later invented miniature glass houses that kept plants alive on long voyages.

MAGIC PLANT
Until the mid-19th century, malaria killed many people every year. During his travels with Humboldt in Peru (above), Bonpland collected samples of the *cinchona* plant. It was subsequently discovered that a substance obtained from the bark of the plant helped treat people who had caught malaria. The substance is quinine.

Sarcococca hookeriana

BEARDED BOTANIST
Sir Joseph Hooker was a leading botanist explorer of the mid- to late 19th century. He took part in Sir James Ross' Antarctic expedition of 1839 and visited parts of Asia, where he collected many new specimens.

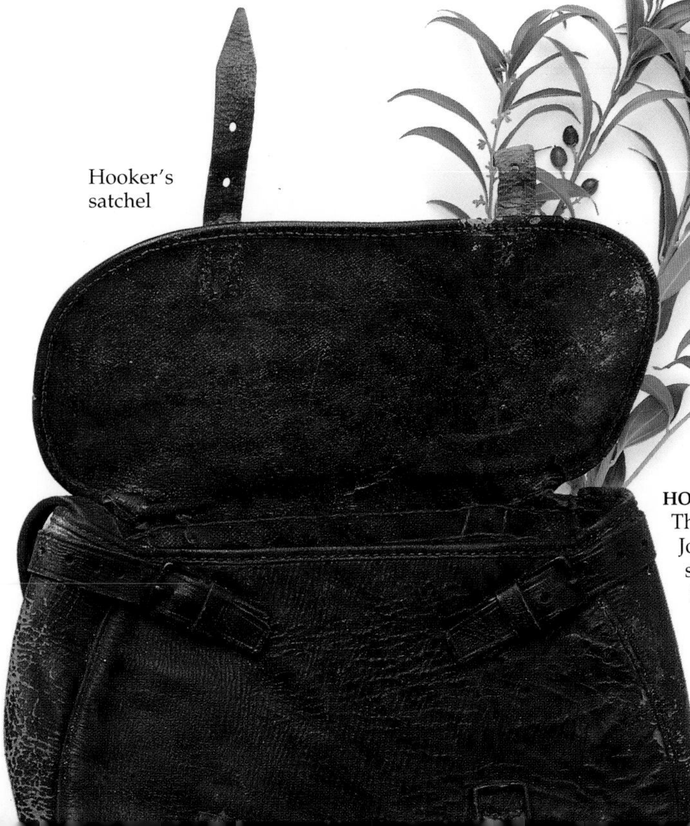

Hooker's satchel

Hevea brasiliense

HOOKER'S BAG
Throughout his long travels, Sir Joseph Hooker wore this leather satchel into which he put interesting plants he found. Several of the new species he discovered were named after him, such as the *Sarcococca hookeriana* shown here.

INTO THE JUNGLE
Naturalist explorers had to penetrate the most inaccessible areas in their quest for new plants.

Pressed eucalyptus leaves

This collection of notes is from Parry's first voyage to the Arctic

Arctic poppy

Arctic moss

FLORA ARCTICA
These notes were written by Sir William Parry in the 19th century. Parry took part in five voyages of exploration to the Arctic between 1818 and 1827 (pp. 52–53) during which time he collected and studied vast numbers of plants. Parry's extensive records brought his explorations to the public's attention.

Pressed hibiscus

BANKS' HIBISCUS
Sir Joseph Banks was the first great naturalist explorer. In 1768, he sailed with Captain Cook to the Pacific Ocean (pp. 34–35). He took with him two botanists, an astronomer, an artist, and four servants. Banks brought back this pressed hibiscus from Polynesia, where its inner bark was used to make "grass" skirts (pp.14–15).

Hibiscus tricuspis

RUBBER PLANT
The rubber plant was originally found by Spanish explorers of South America (pp. 30–33). Local tribes dried the sap of the plant to form bouncing balls which were used in games. This particular species, *Hevea brasiliense*, was discovered by the French scientist Charles Marie de La Condamine. During the 19th century, science found many new uses for rubber, and demand for the plants soared.

51

The North Pole

THE HOSTILE AND DANGEROUS REGIONS of the Arctic (pp. 62–63) were the object of many 19th-century voyages. Explorations were led by naval officers instructed to map the remote regions and to report what they found. The expeditions sailed in bulky ships strong enough to withstand the pressure of ice and packed with enough supplies to last several years. The teams were equipped with a variety of scientific instruments to help them collect rock samples and study wildlife. The men often went ashore on the bleak islands to continue their studies. The long series of expeditions culminated with Robert Peary's success in 1909. Peary was a U.S. Navy officer who had already spent many years in the Arctic. In 1909, he led the first team of men to reach the North Pole.

POLAR PRIZE!
"The Pole at last!," wrote Peary in his diary. "My dream and goal for 20 years." In the late afternoon of April 6, 1909, Robert Peary and his team took the last steps of an agonizing climb to become the first men to reach the North Pole, a huge mass of ice that floats on the Arctic Ocean. The team consisted of his friend, Matthew Henson, and four Inuit (Eskimo) companions, Ooqueah, Ootah, Egingwah, and Seegloo.

ARCTIC TRANSPORT
Polar explorers are faced with the task of transporting supplies and equipment across many miles of snow and ice. Sleds are used for this task. They need to be strong and big enough to carry heavy loads, but light enough to be hauled up slopes and moved by men and dogs.

SEALSKIN CLOTHING
Early Arctic explorers wore European-style wool clothing, which failed to protect them from the Arctic elements. They later learned to wear clothing modeled on local Inuit designs. Sealskin hoods and mittens kept out the coldest winds and saved many an explorer from frostbite.

Tent poles

Sleeping tent for eight men

Tripod for ice saw

Rawhide

Iron-shod runners

Sealskin hood

Sealskin glove

This Boat is left for Captain Parry and his party on their return from attempting to reach the North Pole.

It is particularly requested that she may not be removed, as they will probably be much in want of her.

H.M. Ship Hecla,
May 15th 1827.

PLEASE DO NOT MOVE!
Before the days of radio communication, explorers were often out of touch for months at a time. In 1827, Sir William Parry and a team of men left their ship, the *Hecla*, to set out over land in an attempt to reach the North Pole. The team left this message on board a small boat which they left behind for future use.

SLED HAULING
Loaded sleds were very heavy to pull. The job was shared between teams of husky dogs and the men themselves.

Load protected by canvas cover

Tea kettle

Cooking utensils

Alcohol lamp for cooking

Net for carrying extra luggage

Pickax

Shovel for digging snow

The South Pole

WHILE MANY EXPLORERS continued to be attracted to the Arctic regions, others turned their attention southward – to Antarctica (pp. 62–63), a vast continent where the climate is even harsher than that of the Arctic. Apart from the lure of being first to reach the South Pole, there was a wealth of wildlife to study in the southern oceans, and the rocks of Antarctica were thought to contain fossils and minerals. Several British and Australian naval explorations of Antarctica culminated in the journeys of the two teams led by Captain Robert Scott. The first exploration team, in 1901–1904, gathered vast amounts of scientific data from the coast, while the second, in 1910–1912, was designed to penetrate the interior. Scott led a team of five men to the South Pole, but was beaten by a Norwegian team led by Roald Amundsen. After the Pole had been reached, the focus of exploration shifted to mapping and collecting scientific data. This work continues today.

CROSS-COUNTRY SKIS
Scott used these skis on his first expedition. They are 8 ft (2.5 m) long, wooden, and very heavy!

SNUG AS A BUG
This reindeer-skin sleeping bag belonged to the surgeon on Scott's second expedition. Some of the men slept with the fur inside, others with the fur outside. Whichever way it was used, the reindeer skin was warmer than wool or sheepskin.

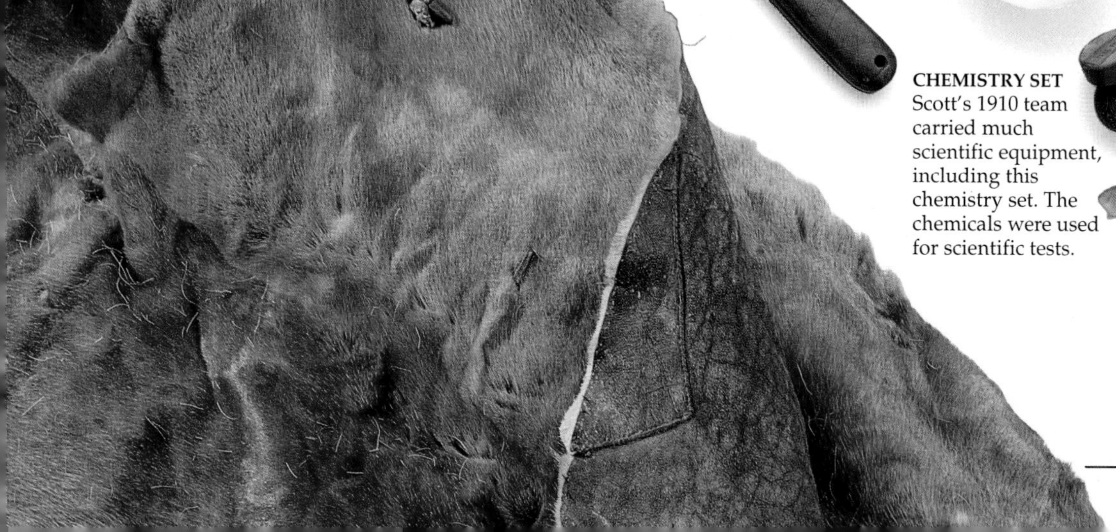

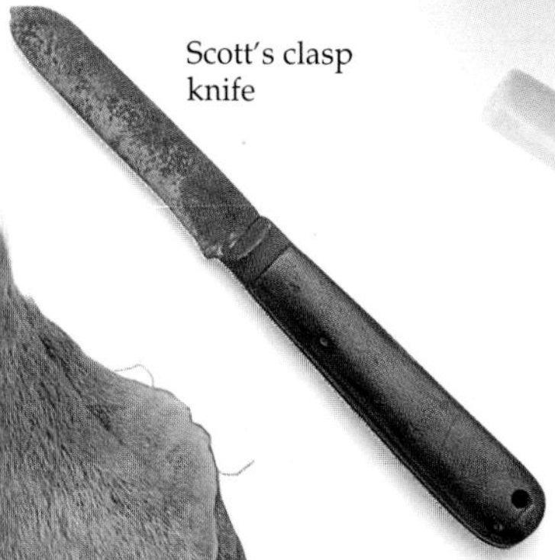

Scott's mug from his first Antarctic voyage

Scott's shaving mirror

Scott's matchbox

Scott's clasp knife

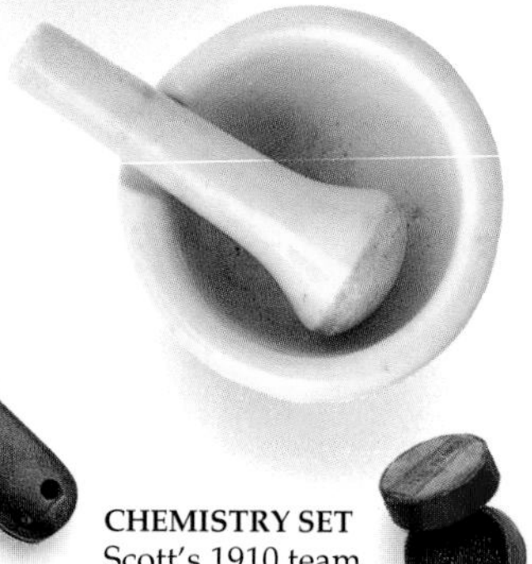

CHEMISTRY SET
Scott's 1910 team carried much scientific equipment, including this chemistry set. The chemicals were used for scientific tests.

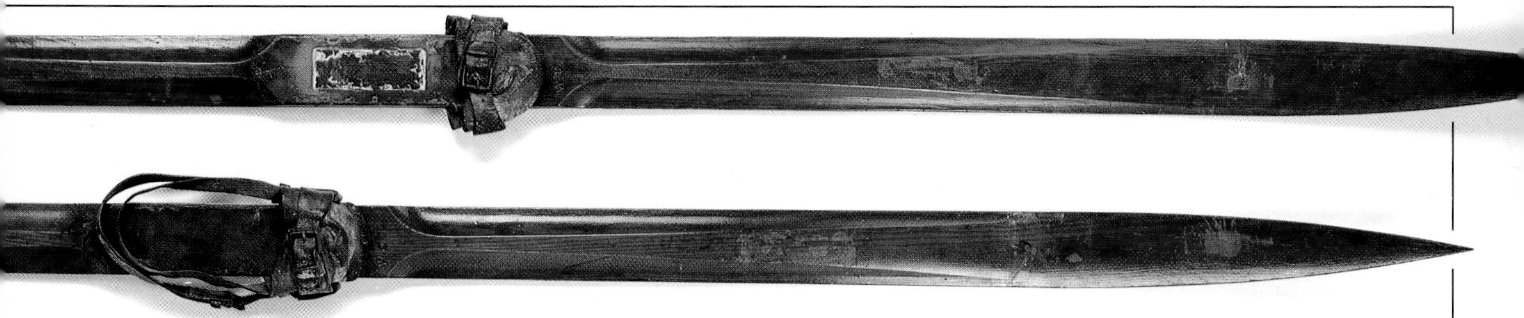

Oates Scott Evans

Bowers Wilson

THE RACE IS LOST

The disappointed and exhausted Scott team reached the South Pole on January 17, 1912. On their desperate struggle back to base, Lawrence Oates, who was very weak and was holding up the team, said "I am just going outside and may be some time." He walked out of the tent into the blizzard and was never seen again. Scott wrote in his journal, "We knew poor Oates was walking to his death." None of the team returned alive.

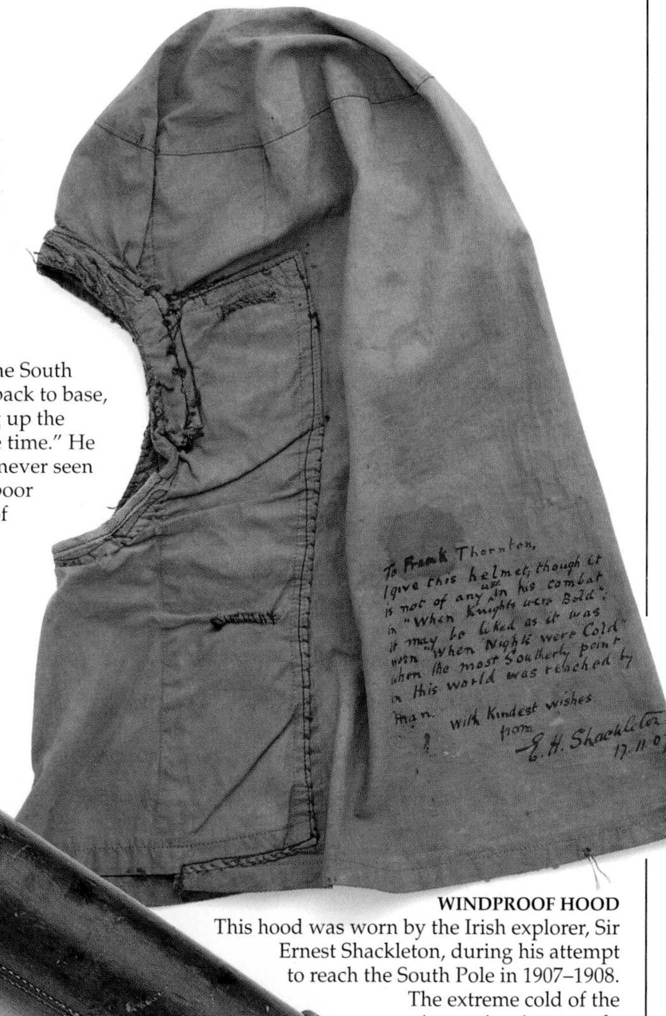

SIGHT-SEEING

This telescope was used by Scott during his expeditions. It was a vital piece of equipment for the men attempting to navigate across vast frozen plains and through mountain passes, since it enabled them to locate the food and fuel caches previously left by the depot-laying parties. These were marked by small cairns with flags fluttering on them.

WINDPROOF HOOD

This hood was worn by the Irish explorer, Sir Ernest Shackleton, during his attempt to reach the South Pole in 1907–1908. The extreme cold of the Antarctic winter made such clothing vital. Shackleton later signed the hood as a presentation gift.

FLYING FLAG

Richard Byrd mapped large areas of land and sea and was one of the first explorers to use an aircraft (pp. 56–57). In 1926 he flew across the North Pole, and in 1929 he flew over the South Pole. This flag was flown from his aircraft as he crossed the Poles.

BYRD'S PLANE

Richard Byrd's plane was called *Josephine*. You can see it here being unloaded from a ship in Spitsbergen (pp. 62–63).

Pioneers of the air

Hᴏᴛ-ᴀɪʀ ᴀɴᴅ ʜʏᴅʀᴏɢᴇɴ balloons were the only way people could fly until the early 20th century. These balloons could not stay aloft for long, and as there was no way to steer them, they traveled with the wind. When the Wright brothers made the first successful engine-powered flight in 1903, they heralded a new era of travel. Many of the early air pioneers were adventurous travelers who either flew across areas never before visited by humans, or who opened up air routes to previously isolated regions. Early aircraft were constructed from wood and fabric and were highly unreliable; many early explorers of the skies were killed when their aircraft broke apart or crashed. By the 1930s, aircraft were being used to map areas of land. Photographs taken from an aircraft accurately showed the landscapes. Today, many maps are completed with the aid of aerial photography. It has even been possible to map inaccessible mountain areas.

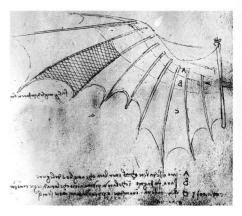

BIRDMAN
This design for an artificial wing – based on a bird's wing – was drawn by Leonardo da Vinci, the great 16th-century Italian artist and scientist. However, his design was doomed to fail as human muscles are not strong enough to power such wings!

LADY OF THE SKIES
In the early 20th century, the world was amazed by the exploits of a young woman named Amy Johnson. In 1930, she flew solo from London to Australia in a record-breaking 19 days. The following year, she flew to Japan over much previously unexplored territory.

Wooden spars to shape and strengthen wing

LIGHT POWER
Early engines were so heavy it was difficult for aircraft to get off the ground. From 1908, new lightweight engines like this one were developed. The overhead valves and light drive shaft and pistons gave it considerable power.

RECORD-BREAKER
Amelia Earhart set many flying records and out-performed many men. She vanished mysteriously over the Pacific Ocean just before the outbreak of World War II.

AMELIA EARHART   LOCKHEED VEGA

AERIAL MAPPING
The ability to fly made it much easier for explorers to produce accurate maps. A photograph such as this taken from the air shows details of terrain that could take many hours to record from the ground. Most modern maps have been carefully checked against aerial surveys.

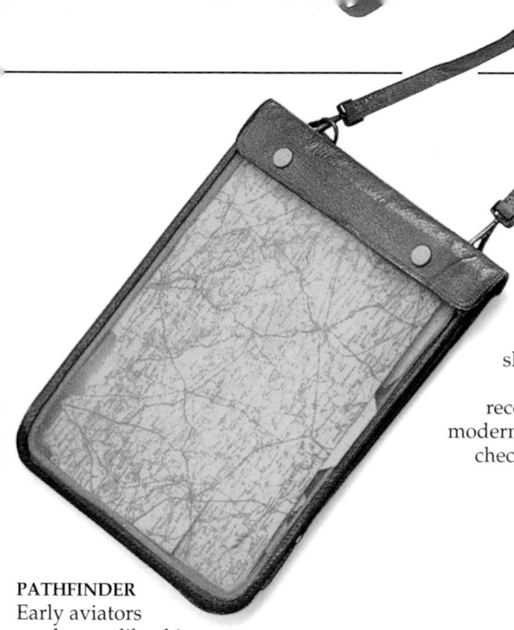

PATHFINDER
Early aviators used maps like this one from World War I to identify landmarks.

Louis Blériot in his monoplane

BLÉRIOT'S MACHINE
The first sea crossing by aircraft was made in 1909 when the French aviation pioneer Louis Blériot flew across the English Channel from Calais to Dover. Blériot flew a lightweight monoplane (a plane with one set of wings) of his own design. The main frame was constructed of wood, over which fabric was stretched.

Air-speed meter

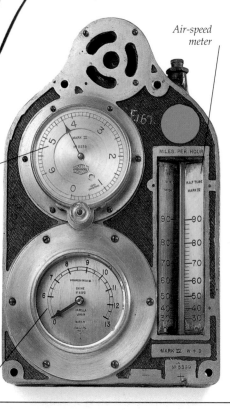

Altimeter

ALONE ACROSS THE ATLANTIC
Aviator Charles Lindbergh was the first person to fly solo across the Atlantic Ocean. He flew from New York to Paris in 1927 and later completed many other pioneering flights. He also surveyed unknown regions from the air, including inland Greenland.

SIMPLE CONTROLS
Modern aircraft are full of high-tech equipment, but early pilots had to make do with very basic controls. This early 20th-century instrument panel contains only an air-speed meter, an altimeter to show the aircraft's height, and a revolution counter to indicate engine speed.

Revolution counter

Into outer space

THE IDEA OF SPACE travel has fired peoples' imaginations for centuries, but it remained a dream until rockets powerful enough to lift objects into space were invented. Such rockets – developed by both the United States and Russia in the mid-20th century – were based on German missiles developed during World War II. The Space Age began in earnest in 1957 when Russia launched *Sputnik 1*, the first artificial satellite to orbit Earth, closely followed by the United States' space satellite *Explorer 1*. The next major step came in 1961 when a man orbited Earth for the first time. The launching of a space shuttle by the United States in 1981 added a further dimension to space exploration; rockets can be used only once, but space shuttles can be used many times. Current space exploration includes the study of the solar system's giant planets to see if they are capable of supporting human life.

An imaginary view of Mars!

Capsule

Rocket

INTO SPACE
Years of work by the Russian scientist Sergey Korolyov resulted in a rocket that could carry a human into orbit. Yuri Gagarin was launched into space on April 12th, 1961. His historic journey lasted less than two hours, during which time he completed one orbit of the Earth.

Upper section

Hatch

Lower section

THE *VOSTOK* ROCKET
Yuri Gagarin was launched into space in a *Vostock* capsule about 8 ft (2.5 m) in diameter. A huge disposable rocket made up of four cone-shaped booster rockets attached to a central core rocket – and 13 times as big as the capsule – was necessary to launch him and the capsule into orbit.

SPACE SPIDER
On July 20th, 1969, the first man landed on the moon in this lunar module, which contained scientific equipment designed to study the moon's surface. Automatic television cameras sent back live pictures of the moment Neil Armstrong climbed down the ladder and said the words "That's one small step for a man, one giant leap for mankind."

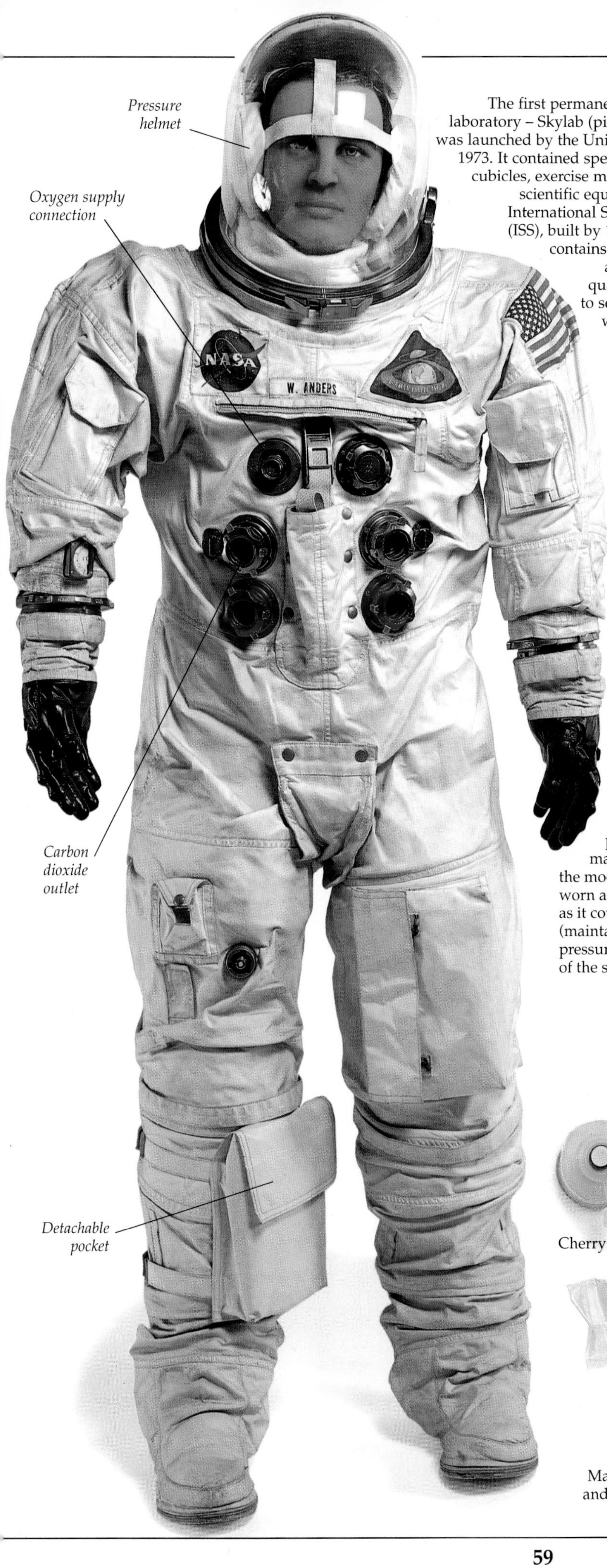

Pressure
helmet

Oxygen supply
connection

SPACE LABORATORIES
The first permanent orbiting science laboratory – Skylab (pictured right) – was launched by the United States in 1973. It contained special sleeping cubicles, exercise machines, and scientific equipment. The International Space Station (ISS), built by 16 countries, contains laboratories and sleeping quarters for up to seven people, who will live and work in space.

SPACEWALKING
This astronaut is floating freely in space. His backpack contains small thruster rockets that enable him to move around and change direction. Earlier spacewalkers were attached to their spacecraft by lifelines. "Floating" astronauts are helping to build the ISS in space.

SPACE CLOTHES
This spacesuit was worn by astronaut William Anders, pilot of the first manned flight around the moon in 1968. It was worn as a safety measure as it could be pressurized (maintained at normal air pressure) independently of the spacecraft.

Carbon
dioxide
outlet

Detachable
pocket

MISSION FOOD
As soon as space flights began to last more than a few hours, the problem of food and drink had to be solved. To save weight, many space foods are freeze-dried or dehydrated (water removed). Astronauts use the water produced during the generating of electricity to re-hydrate their meals. The food below came from U.S. and Russian space missions.

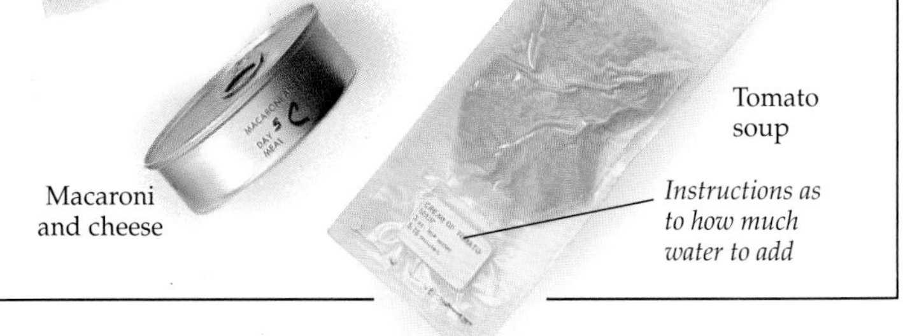

Chocolate
pudding

Cherry drink

Dried
bread
cubes

Tomato
soup

Macaroni
and cheese

Instructions as
to how much
water to add

Exploring the deep

Nearly three-quarters of the Earth's surface is covered by water, but it is only relatively recently that the mysterious world beneath the waves has been properly explored. The first official expedition to investigate this underwater world was in 1872 when the ship *Challenger* was equipped with scientific instruments to gather information from the ocean depths. The introduction in the first half of the 20th century of "bathyscaphes," vehicles that could dive beneath the surface, was the next major development in underwater exploration. These enabled scientists to explore deeper than had previously been possible. As a result of the ever-increasing sophistication of diving vehicles and equipment, and the subsequent surge in underwater exploration, we now know that the lands beneath the oceans include mountain ranges, valleys, and plains similar to those we are familiar with on dry land.

Mermaids – mythical creatures, half human and half fish, that live beneath the ocean waves – are said to attract men by their beauty and singing

DIVING SHIP
Auguste Piccard and his son Jacques designed this bathyscaphe called *Trieste* to work at great depths. In 1960, Jacques took it down to 7 miles (11 km). The hull had to be very strong to withstand the pressure at such a great depth.

HEAVY AIR
Salvaging items from shipwrecks in shallow water has always been profitable. However, this activity used to be limited by the length of time a diver could hold his breath. In 1819, Augustus Siebe invented a copper diving helmet (left) that allowed divers to work at a depth of 197 ft (60 m) for longer periods of time. A crew on the surface pumped air down a long pipe attached to the helmet. The diver had to be careful not to damage the pipe as this could cut off his air supply.

Helmet is made of copper and weighs approximately 20 lb (9 kg)

TRIESTE

Steel ball in which crew traveled

FREEDOM!
In 1943, French naval officer Jacques-Yves Cousteau helped to invent the "aqualung," a device that automatically supplies air to divers from bottles strapped to their backs.

LOCATING OIL
The Seatask submersible is used in the search for oil. Divers can work in normal air pressure in the upper chamber. They have to put on helmets when they leave to explore the sea bed.

WRECK SALVAGING
Observation chambers like this were used around the 1930s to survey wrecks. They were built to withstand the external water pressure at great depths and were equipped with an air regeneration system.

Diver climbs in here

UNDERWATER SPACESUITS
Modern divers often wear one-man armored suits like this for scientific exploration and for work around oil rigs. These suits are strong enough to withstand water pressure – and retain normal air pressure inside – at depths of up to 600 ft (200 m).

SEA BED DISCOVERIES *below*
Shipwrecks are fascinating to explore, both for the archeologist and the naturalist. They are a source of both treasures from the past, like this pot, and of marine wildlife.

Exploration routes

THIS GLOBAL MAP shows the routes of some of the most important explorers mentioned in this book. As you can see, early explorers traveled only relatively short distances, but as technology improved, the intrepid men and women who followed in the early travelers' footsteps were able to cover ever-larger areas. Many of them made detailed maps and notes of the areas they explored, and it is because of the information they gathered that we know so much about the world we live in.

18th-century explorers of North America saw polar bears like this one painted by naturalist explorer John Audubon (pp. 44–45)

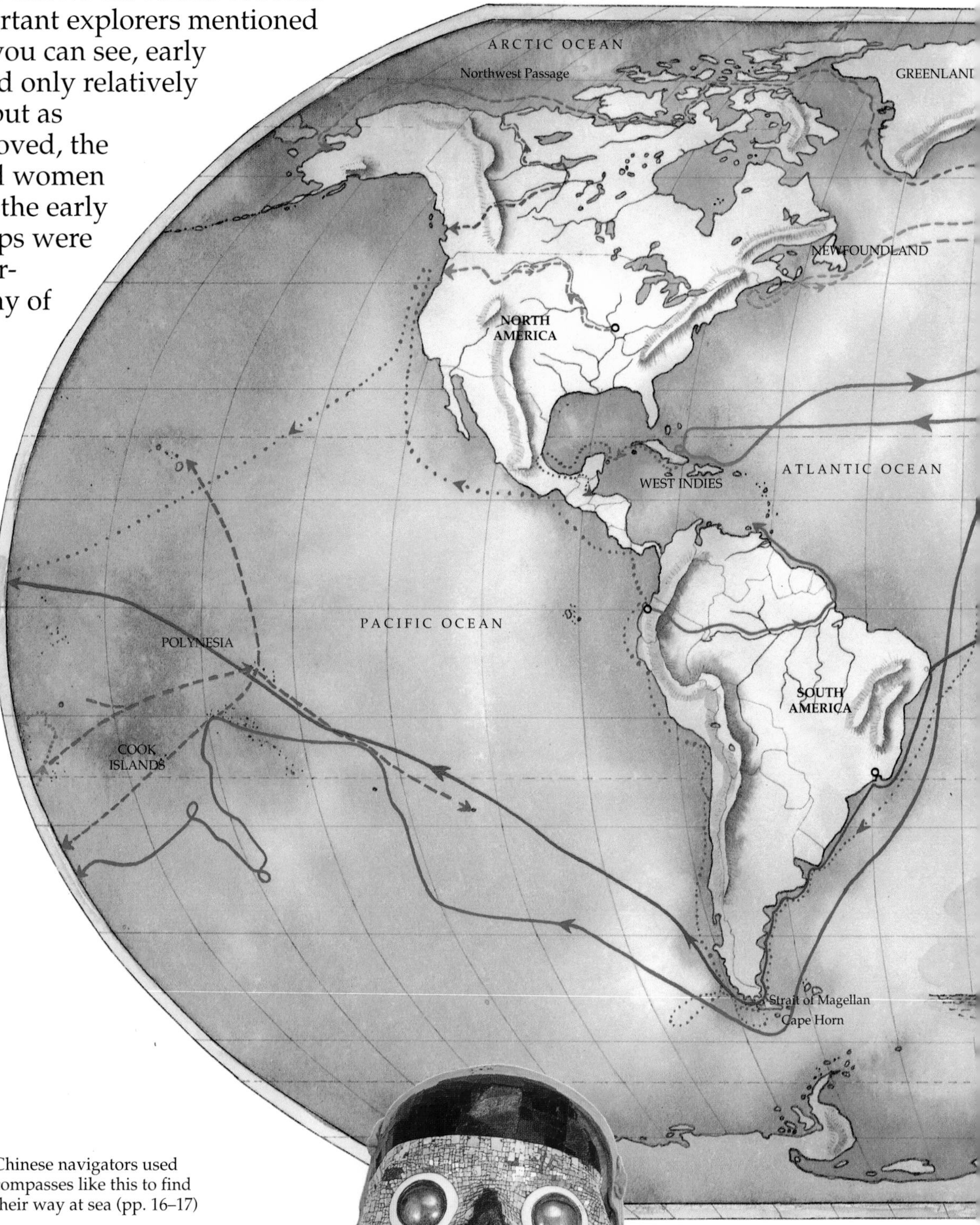

ARCTIC OCEAN

Northwest Passage

GREENLAND

NEWFOUNDLAND

NORTH AMERICA

ATLANTIC OCEAN

WEST INDIES

PACIFIC OCEAN

POLYNESIA

SOUTH AMERICA

COOK ISLANDS

Strait of Magellan
Cape Horn

Chinese navigators used compasses like this to find their way at sea (pp. 16–17)

Spanish explorers of South America returned home with "souvenirs" like this mask of the Aztec god Tezcatlipoca (pp. 30–31). The mask is made from the skull of a victim sacrificed to the god, with white shells for teeth and polished iron pyrite for the eyes.

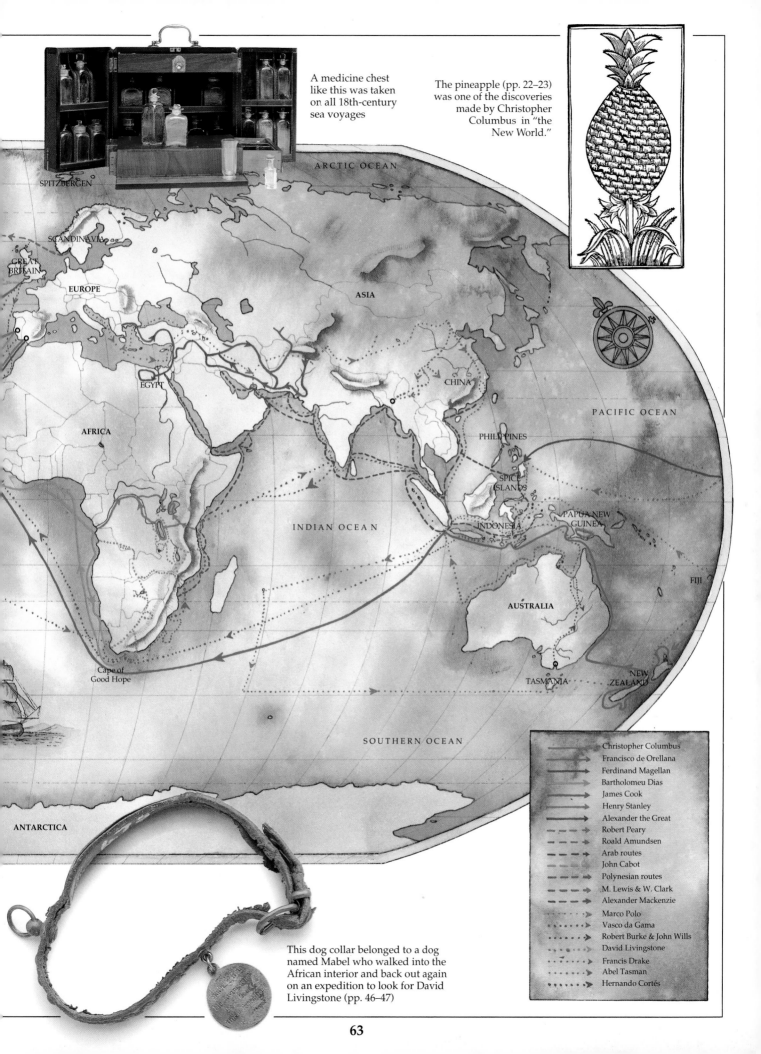

A medicine chest like this was taken on all 18th-century sea voyages

The pineapple (pp. 22–23) was one of the discoveries made by Christopher Columbus in "the New World."

ARCTIC OCEAN

SPITZBERGEN

SCANDINAVIA

GREAT BRITAIN

EUROPE

ASIA

CHINA

PACIFIC OCEAN

EGYPT

AFRICA

PHILIPPINES

SPICE ISLANDS

INDONESIA

PAPUA NEW GUINEA

INDIAN OCEAN

AUSTRALIA

FIJI

Cape of Good Hope

TASMANIA

NEW ZEALAND

SOUTHERN OCEAN

ANTARCTICA

This dog collar belonged to a dog named Mabel who walked into the African interior and back out again on an expedition to look for David Livingstone (pp. 46–47)

Christopher Columbus
Francisco de Orellana
Ferdinand Magellan
Bartholomeu Dias
James Cook
Henry Stanley
Alexander the Great
Robert Peary
Roald Amundsen
Arab routes
John Cabot
Polynesian routes
M. Lewis & W. Clark
Alexander Mackenzie
Marco Polo
Vasco da Gama
Robert Burke & John Wills
David Livingstone
Francis Drake
Abel Tasman
Hernando Cortés

Did you know?

AMAZING FACTS

Early explorers had to face terrifying myths and legends, such as stories of huge sea monsters that swam in uncharted waters (probaby based on whale sightings).

In the 1400s, some Portuguese sailors who set out to explore the coast of Africa believed that the sea would boil as they neared the equator.

Sea monster on 1619 map

The Norwegian Viking explorer Floki Vilgerdarson (later nicknamed Raven-Floki) carried three ravens (sacred to the Viking god Odin) on board his ship to guide him. Each time he released a bird, it returned to the ship. Then, one day, a raven flew forward. Floki followed it and discovered the coast of Iceland.

After Bartolomeu Diaz sailed around the southern tip of Africa in 1488, he called it Cabo Tormentoso or the Cape of Storms. The point was renamed Cabo da Boa Esperanca (the Cape of Good Hope) by King John II of Portugal.

On his voyage of 1497–98, Vasco da Gama's ships carried large stone crosses called padroes, which were positioned on high land near the sea.

Amerigo Vespucci, the Italian trader and navigator, not only gave his name to America – he was also the first to use the phrase "Mundus Novus," or "New World," in a letter about the discovery.

When Columbus sailed across the Atlantic in 1492, he believed he had reached islands off Japan and China and called them the "Indies," the old European name for Asia. He died believing he had been the first European to find a western route to Asia, not the first to reach America.

Newly claimed lands were often named after their royal patrons, so the English colony of Virginia in North America was named in honor of Queen Elizabeth I, the Virgin Queen, and Louisiana for the French king, Louis XIV.

After Cortés had decided to invade the Aztec Empire with a force of just 508 soldiers and 100 sailors, he burned his ships so there was no turning back. His men would see victory – or death.

Banksia serrata, gathered from Botany Bay, Australia, on Captain Cook's first voyage

French newspaper cartoon of Peary's dispute

Magellan's ships were the first European ships to sail into the Pacific Ocean. However, Vasco de Balboa was the first European to see the Pacific, after crossing Central America on foot from east to west in 1513.

Balboa called the Pacific the "Great South Sea," but Magellan named it "Pacific" because of its peaceful winds.

Naturalists on Cook's voyage to the Pacific in 1768 collected so many specimens in one bay in Australia that Cook named it Botany Bay.

Cook's reports of rich sea life in the unexplored Southern Ocean in the early 1770s attracted hundreds of sealers and whalers to the area, who almost hunted fur seals and the southern right whale to extinction.

Although linked forever as a pair of famous explorers, Henry Stanley and David Livingstone met only once and spent just a few months together.

European explorers in Africa didn't travel light. Many had over 50 African porters to carry their equipment.

After Robert Peary returned from the Arctic in 1909, he was furious to learn that Frederick Cook was claiming he had reached the North Pole a year earlier. Congress later backed Peary's claim.

One of Vasco da Gama's padroes at Malindi, Kenya, used to claim land for Portugal

QUESTIONS AND ANSWERS

Q Who first crossed the Atlantic?

A For many years, people believed Columbus was the first to make the voyage, in 1492, when he sighted one of the islands of the present-day Bahamas, naming it San Salvador. However, there is evidence to prove that the journey was made around 500 years earlier by the Vikings. Settler Bjarni Herjolfsson is said to have sighted the coast of Labrador in 985, when drifting off course on a voyage to Greenland. Leif Erikson, another Viking, became North America's first recorded European explorer when he set foot on the east coast of North America 15 years later, in 1000. Leif named the land that he discovered "Vinland."

Q How did early explorers sail without instruments of navigation?

A Before the invention of instruments of navigation, explorers sailed by intelligent guesswork, using their knowledge of winds and ocean currents to estimate distance and direction. In unknown waters, clues such as driftwood and the presence of certain seabirds suggested land was close. For example, the frigate bird does not land on water, so if they saw one, sailors knew they must be nearing land.

Q Who discovered the secret of latitude?

A Latitude (north-south position) was first measured by ancient Greek scientists in the third century B.C.E., using a scaphe, or hollow sundial. The Greeks also invented the astrolabe and Greek geographers were the first to draw lines of latitude on maps.

Q Why was the discovery of longitude so important?

A Although early seafarers could find their latitude from the sun and stars, they had to use dead reckoning (keeping records of the distance and direction traveled each day) to work out their longitude, or east-west position. Since it was easy to make mistakes, voyages were potentially dangerous and mapping was inaccurate. By the time James Cook went on his second voyage in 1772, however, he could find his longitude with a highly accurate clock called a chronometer, designed by the ingenious clockmaker John Harrison just a few years before.

Himalayas in central Asia

Frigate bird

Q Why was the African interior unexplored by Europeans for so long?

A Mainly because it was dangerous! Tropical disease could kill a European within a day. There were savage wild animals, such as lions and crocodiles, and explorers had to contend with a variety of unknown landscapes from empty desert, to swamps and thick rain forests.

Q Were all explorers' tales true?

A It must have been tempting for some explorers to exaggerate tales of strange places. Although many did not believe Marco Polo when he spoke of Eastern springs that gushed black oil, he was, in fact, describing the Baku oilfields in modern-day Azerbaijan.

Q Is there anywhere on Earth left to explore?

A Today, there is almost no place left on Earth still unknown and unnamed. We know what lies at the top of the highest mountains and, for the most part, in the ocean's deepest depths. As distant places become more familiar, the nature of exploration has changed. Rather than seek out the world's wild places, the challenge for explorers today is to try to understand the Earth and preserve its wonders for future generations.

Record Breakers

FIRST TO SAIL AROUND AFRICA
The Phoenicians are thought to have sailed around the tip of Africa from Egypt via the Red Sea on behalf of the Egyptian pharaoh Neco (610–595 B.C.).

FIRST EUROPEAN TO SAIL AROUND AFRICA
Bartolomeu Diaz sailed around the southern tip of Africa in 1488 after a fierce storm drove his ships out of sight of land.

FIRST TO SAIL AROUND THE WORLD
Ferdinand Magellan's expedition to find a westward route to Asia ended with one of five ships, the *Vittoria*, returning to Spain.

LONGEST TRANSCONTINENTAL JOURNEY
Meriwether Lewis and William Clark traveled across North America to the Pacific Ocean in 1804–06.

FIRST EUROPEAN TO FIND THE SOURCE OF THE NILE
John Hanning Speke discovered Lake Victoria in 1858 and believed it to be the source of the Nile. Returning in 1862 with James Grant, he finally found the point where the Nile flowed out of the lake.

FIRST TO SAIL THE NORTHWEST PASSAGE
The Norwegian explorer Roald Amundsen was the first person to navigate the Northwest Passage, sailing it from east to west from 1902–06.

FIRST TO REACH THE NORTH POLE
Robert Peary made eight Arctic voyages, reaching the North Pole on April 6, 1909. However, many people still dispute his claim.

FIRST TO REACH THE SOUTH POLE
Roald Amundsen reached the South Pole in December 1911, one month ahead of Captain Scott.

Timeline of explorers

IN THE PAST, EXPLORERS TRAVELED to distant, unknown lands because of trade, conquest, and settlement. Today's explorers, however, are often inspired by adventure or scientific research. Some explorers, such as the Polynesians who sailed across the Pacific, are little known to us because they left no written records of their journeys. The entries below describe the travels of some of the world's great explorers and the dates of their remarkable achievements.

C. 500 B.C.E. HANNO
Phoenician; sailed from Carthage down the coast of West Africa and up the Senegal River, looking for suitable sites for Phoenician colonies

399–414 FA HSIEN
Chinese; Buddhist monk who traveled across Asia on the Silk Road into India and across the sea to Sri Lanka

629–654 HSÜAN TSANG (OR XUAN ZANG)
Chinese; Buddist monk who followed Fa Hsien's route

800–1100 VIKING TRAVELLERS
Crossed the North Atlantic. Erik the Red founded settlements in Greenland. His son, Leif Erikson, founded others on the eastern coast of North America.

1260–71 POLO BROTHERS, NICCOLO AND MAFFEO, AND NICCOLO'S SON, MARCO
Venetian; traveled across Asia to China. Marco Polo remained in China for almost 20 years, working for the Chinese emperor, Kublai Khan.

1324–53 IBN BATTUTA
North African (from Tangier); traveled through the Sahara to Mali and Timbuktu, explored the Middle East and Arabia, and also visited India, Sumatra, and China

1487–88 BARTOLEMEU DIAZ
Portuguese; sailed down the West African coast past the Cape of Good Hope and entered the Indian Ocean

1492–1504 CHRISTOPHER COLUMBUS
Italian; sailed across the Atlantic to the West Indies and, on later voyages, to the coasts of Central and South America

1497–98 JOHN CABOT
Italian, backed by English merchants; reached Newfoundland and the American mainland in search of the Northwest Passage

1497–98 VASCO DA GAMA
Portuguese; sailed down the West African coast, around the Cape of Good Hope, and across the Indian Ocean to India

1519–22 FERDINAND MAGELLAN
Portuguese, backed by Spain; set off to reach the Spice Islands with five ships – one returned after circumnavigating the globe. Magellan himself was killed in the Philippines in 1521.

1519–21 HERNANDO CORTÉS
Spanish; conquered the Aztec Empire for Spain

1531–33 FRANCISCO PIZARRO
Spanish; conquered the Inca Empire for Spain

1534–42 JACQUES CARTIER
French; made three voyages of discovery to North America searching for a western route to Asia

1576 MARTIN FROBISHER
English; reached Baffin Island in search of the Northwest Passage

1577–80 FRANCIS DRAKE
English; circumnavigated the globe in his ship the Golden Hinde, plundering Spanish ships along the way

1594–97 WILLEM BARENTS
Dutch explorer; reached the Kara Sea in search of a Northeast Passage

Christopher Columbus

1607–11 HENRY HUDSON
English; made four voyages searching for both a northeast and northwest passage to Asia; discovered the Hudson River and Hudson Bay, where he died after his crew mutinied and cast him adrift

1603–15 SAMUEL DE CHAMPLAIN
French; founder of French Canada who mapped much of the country's interior

1612–16 WILLIAM BAFFIN
English; navigator who discovered Baffin Bay, Ellesmere Island, and Baffin Island

1642–44 ABEL JANSZOON TASMAN
Dutch; sailed from Mauritius in the Indian Ocean to Tasmania, New Zealand, Fiji, New Guinea, then went on to Papua New Guinea and Java

1678–80 ROBERT CAVELIER, SIEUR DE LA SALLE
French; explored the Great Lakes of North America and sailed down the Mississippi River to the Gulf of Mexico; died trying to find the Mississippi delta from the sea

Charles de la Condamine

Louis Bougainville

1725–29, 1734–41 VITUS BERING
Danish, appointed by the Czar of Russia;
crossed Asia by land to discover whether
Russia and America were joined

1735–44 CHARLES DE LA CONDAMINE
French; first French explorer to sail around
the world; explored the Amazon River

1766–69 LOUIS BOUGAINVILLE
French; sailed from the Falklands across the
Pacific to the Great Barrier Reef on the coast
of Australia, then went on to Java; first
French explorer to sail around the world

1768–79 JAMES COOK
English; made three voyages around the
Pacific, extensively mapping the southern
Pacific and its islands

1795–97, 1805–06 MUNGO PARK
Scottish; reached the Niger River in West
Africa and later explored it upstream

Henry Morton Stanley

1799–1804 ALEXANDER VON HUMBOLDT
German; naturalist who explored
northwest South America

**1804–06 MERIWETHER LEWIS AND
WILLIAM CLARK**
American; sent by President Thomas
Jefferson to find a route westward from
St. Louis to the Pacific Ocean. Their
route took them along the Missouri,
Yellowstone, and Columbia Rivers
by canoe.

1819–27 WILLIAM PARRY
English; commanded five expeditions
to the Arctic, discovering part of the
Northwest Passage

1827–28 RENÉ CAILLIÉ
French; explored region surrounding the
Sahara in West Africa; first European to
visit Timbuktu and survive

1831–35 CHARLES DARWIN
English; explored South America and the
Galapagos Islands, where he gathered
information that formed his theory of
evolution by natural selection

Ranulph Fiennes

1839 JAMES CLARK ROSS
English; explored Antarctic coast and ice
sheets by ship, also searched for John
Franklin (see below)

1828–30, 1844–45 CHARLES STURT
English; mapped the Murray and Darling
Rivers and explored central Australia

1840–41 EDWARD EYRE
English; found land route along the south
coast of Australia from Adelaide to Albany

1841–73 DAVID LIVINGSTONE
Scottish; made four expeditions into Africa,
crossing southern Africa and traveling
south to Cape Town and Port Elizabeth

1844–45, 1850–55 HEINRICH BARTH
German; traveled in West Africa and across
the Sahara

1845–47 JOHN FRANKLIN
English; disappeared on his third voyage
searching for the Northwest Passage

1854–57 RICHARD FRANCIS BURTON
English; traveled with Speke in search
of the source of the Nile

1854–1860 JOHN HANNING SPEKE
English; discovered Lake Victoria in 1858,
then the source of the Nile in 1860

1860–61 ROBERT O'HARA BURKE
Irish; traveled to northern Australia from
Melbourne; died of starvation on the return
journey

1861–61 JOHN STUART
Scottish; crossed Australia from south to
north, from Adelaide to Darwin

1888, 1894–96 FRIDTJOF NANSEN
Norwegian; made first crossing of
Greenland cap ice, deliberately allowing
his ship to become frozen in the pack ice
and then drifting across the Arctic Ocean,
proving the existence of Arctic currents

1871–89 HENRY MORTON STANLEY
American; made three expeditions
across Africa and up the Congo River
in central Africa, finding the "missing"
Scottish explorer and missionary
David Livingstone

1907–09 ERNEST SHACKLETON
Irish; traveled to within 100 miles (160 km)
of the South Pole

1908–09 ROBERT PEARY
American; claimed to reach the North Pole
after eight expeditions to the Arctic. Even
though Congress backed his claim, many
doubt that Peary reached the pole

1910–12 ROALD AMUNDSEN
Norwegian; first to sail the Northwest
Passage; first to reach the South Pole, using
sleds pulled by dogs

1910–13 ROBERT FALCON SCOTT
English; just beaten to the South Pole by
Amundsen. The four-man team died on the
return journey.

1961 YURI GAGARIN
Russian cosmonaut; first man in space

1963 VALENTINA TERESHKOVA
Russian cosmonaut; first woman in space

1965 ALEKSEI LEONOV
Russian cosmonaut; first person to
"walk" in space.

1969 NEIL ARMSTRONG
American astronaut; first man to set foot
on the moon, followed by Buzz Aldrin

JACQUES-YVES COUSTEAU
French ocean explorer; helped invent the
aqualung in 1943 and assisted Piccard in
developing the bathyscaphe

1960 JACQUES PICCARD
Swiss undersea explorer; accompanied
by Don Walsh, made the deepest-ever
manned dive, almost 7 miles (11 km) into
the Mariana Trench in the Pacific Ocean,
in the *Trieste*

1977 ROBERT BALLARD
American oceanographer and explorer;
accompanied by John Corliss, discovered
hydrothermal vents 8,202 ft (2,500 m) deep
in the Pacific Ocean

1968–69 WALLY HERBERT
English; led first dogsled journey across
the Arctic Ocean via the North Pole

1992–93 RANULPH FIENNES
English; made the first unsupported
crossing of Antarctica, with Mike Stroud

Jacques Piccard

Find out more

TODAY, LITTLE OF OUR WORLD remains unknown, and television brings faraway places into our homes. It is therefore difficult to imagine what it must have been like for the early explorers who did not know what they would find when they journeyed to distant lands. Watch for television programs and movies that bring the journeys of various explorers to life. Check out nearby museums to see if they have collections related to exploration, or use the internet to take a virtual tour of museums housing artifacts used by explorers.

Astrolabe

ARABIC ASTROLABES
Some museums, including England's National Maritime Museum at Greenwich, have collections of early navigation instruments, such as sextants, compasses, and astrolabes.

Replica ship Endeavour in full sail

PAINTINGS
Many art galleries and museums display portraits of some of the great explorers and paintings of their journeys. The painting above is by William Hodges, an artist on Captain James Cook's second voyage, and is called *Tahitian War Galleys in Matavai Bay, Tahiti* (1766). Look for dramatic photographs from more recent expeditions (such as the trans-Antarctic crossing undertaken by Ranulph Fiennes and Mike Stroud in 1992–93, or the launching of probes to explore space), which are often printed in newspapers or shown on television news.

USEFUL WEB SITES

- Home page of the Mariner's Museum in Newport, Virginia, with plenty of information on exploration, including biographies:
  www.mariner.org
- Interactive exhibit on Lewis and Clark and the 1804 journey of the Corps of Discovery across America:
  www.lewisandclarkexhibit.org
- Web site devoted to the life and voyages of Captain Cook:
  www.captaincooksociety.com
- To go on a virtual exploration of the world's oceans:
  www.divediscover.whoi.edu
- For information about exploring space for radio signals:
  setiathome.ssl.berkeley.edu

GET ON BOARD
Several re-creations of sailing ships have been built. For example, a replica of Cook's ship, the *Endeavour*, was built at Fremantle in Australia between 1988 and 1994, following official plans and using many 18th-century methods. Today, the ship sails to different countries and you can actually book a day's voyage on board. Check out the official web site on www.barkendeavour.com.au for the latest information. The re-created ship was also the subject of a 2002 BBC documentary called *The Ship*, in which people re-created one of Cook's voyages to the Pacific.

*Sign marking
the Lewis and
Clark Trail*

WALK THE LEWIS AND CLARK TRAIL
The years 2003–06 mark the 200th anniversary of Meriwether Lewis and William Clark's epic journey across North America. Some of the journey (which started at Camp DuBois in Illinois, then continued up the Missouri River, over the Rocky Mountains, down the Snake and Columbia Rivers to the Pacific Ocean) can be walked on the Lewis and Clark National Historic Trail, which passes through 11 states. Log on to the web site at www.lewisandclark.org to find out more.

*The Endeavour
space shuttle
blasts into space*

GO EXPLORING
Through the Internet, it's possible to link up to current voyages of exploration to deepsea hydro-thermal vents or mid-ocean ridges. If you are interested in space exploration, browse the web site at http://spaceflight.nasa.gov, which has information on all the latest shuttle missions, or even take a trip to see a shuttle launch. You could also join the SETI@home project – a radio exploration of space to search for extraterrestrial intelligence run by the University of Berkeley.

Shuttle launch at the
Kennedy Space Center,
Cape Canaveral, Florida

DARWIN CENTRE
The Darwin Centre opened at the Natural History Museum in London in 2002 and houses 22 million preserved animal specimens. Visitors can tour 17 miles (27 km) of shelving, which holds glass vessels containing creatures collected from all over the world during the past 300 years. The collection includes snakes, baby crocodiles, and other finds collected during Captain Cook's first voyage to Australia in the 1770s.

Places to visit

**MARITIME MUSEUM OF SAN DIEGO,
SAN DIEGO, CALIFORNIA**
(619) 234-9153
www.sdmaritime.com
The museum displays the *Star of India,* the world's oldest active ship; the *California,* a replica of a mid-19th century revenue cutter; and three other historic ships. Exhibits include the Age of Sail, the Age of Steam, and Charting the Sea.

**KENNEDY SPACE CENTER,
CAPE CANAVERAL, FLORIDA**
www.kennedyspacecenter.com
Visit the space center and see launch pads, rockets, historic technology, and real space hardware. Experience the excitement of the Apollo moon program. Touch a real piece of Mars. There's even an interactive space flight simulator!

THE SANTA MARIA, COLUMBUS, OHIO
(614) 645-8760
www.santamaria.org
In the city named after him, you'll find a life-size replica of Christopher Columbus's flagship. Tours dramatize the daring of the explorer and his crew. An overnight program lets visitors sleep on board.

**MISSOURI HISTORICAL SOCIETY,
ST. LOUIS, MISSOURI**
(314) 361-7395
www.mohistory.org
A great collection on Lewis and Clark's Corps of Discovery, including journals, maps, scientific specimens, and Indian artifacts.

**NATIONAL MARITIME MUSEUM,
GREENWICH, ENGLAND**
www.nmm.ac.uk
This is the largest maritime museum in the world, with galleries dedicated to the history of exploration and how it shaped the world. There are also many paintings on display. Highlights include navigational instruments, such as James Cook's sextant and John Harrison's first marine timekeeper for finding longitude, as well as examples of atlases, maps, and charts, including a vellum Portuguese manuscript chart of the North Atlantic, created around 1535.

**THE BRITISH MUSEUM,
LONDON, ENGLAND**
www.britishmuseum.ac.uk
The museum has thousands of objects from different cultures. Look for Chinese porcelain and jade in the China, South, and Southeast Asia gallery, as well as models of ships in the Egyptian galleries.

Ming porcelain
pot on display
at the British
Museum

Glossary

ASTROLABE (see also SEAMAN'S ASTROLABE) Navigational instrument used by the ancient Greeks and others to measure the height of the sun or stars above the horizon; from the Greek words astrer (star) and labin (to take)

BACKSTAFF (see also CROSS-STAFF) Navigational instrument with a crossbar for sighting (like a cross-staff), and two circular arcs at either end. To take a measurement, the observer turned his back to the sun, so the sun's rays passed through the slot of the sight on the upper arc and hit the arc at the end of the rod. Invented by Captain John Davis in 1595 as a way of measuring latitude without risking the observer's eyesight by staring at the sun.

BALLAST Heavy material, such as concrete, stones, or lead, placed low down in a ship to increase its stability

CARAVEL Small, light, three-masted ship usually rigged with lateen sails, designed by Portuguese shipbuilders in the 14th century; often known as the explorer's ship

CARAVELLA REDONDA (see also CARAVEL) Caravel rigged with square sails

CARRACK (see also NAO) Northern European name for a type of ship known by Spanish and Portuguese as a Nao

CARTHAGE One of the most important Phoenician colonies, in North Africa (near present-day Tunis)

Dhow

CARTOGRAPHER Mapmaker

CARTOGRAPHY The science and art of projecting part of the Earth's surface onto a flat plane

CARTOUCHE Oval shape in which Egyptian characters representing a ruler's name were written

CINCHONA Plant from which quinine is obtained; used by explorers to ease the symptoms of malaria

COMPASS (see also LODESTONE) Navigational instrument used by mariners in which a magnetized metal needle aligns itself with the Earth's magnetic fields; invented by the Chinese more than 2000 years ago

CROSS-STAFF (see also BACKSTAFF) Simple navigational instrument used to measure a ship's latitude. The navigator lined up the crossbar between the sun or pole star and the horizon, then read off the angle of the sun or star from the horizon, enabling him to calculate the ship's distance from the equator.

DEAD RECKONING A navigational method based on keeping records of the distance and direction sailed from a known point, such as a port

DHOW Sailing ship with triangular lateen sails rigged on one or two masts; used for hundreds of years by Muslim traders in the Persian Gulf and Indian Ocean

EL DORADO Spanish for "The Golden One," or a king dusted with gold; came to mean a legendary city of gold, sought by Spanish explorers and others in Central and South America

ENDEAVOUR Captain James Cook's ship on his voyage to the Pacific in 1768–71. The *Endeavour* was a cat collier from Whitby, England, armed with six carriage guns and eight swivel guns with a large storage hold. The ship was broken up in 1793.

GOLDEN HINDE Francis Drake's ship on his circumnavigation of the globe (1577–80)

HARDTACK A type of biscuit that lasted for years, often taken on long sea voyages

JADE (see also SILK ROAD) Hard, ornamental stone of varying colors, often green, prized in China, Mexico, and South America. Chinese carvings made of jade were often traded down the Silk Road.

JUNK Large Chinese sailing ship with a flat bottom, usually used to carry cargo

KNARR (or KNORR) (see also LONGSHIP) Large Viking ship that sat deeper in the water than a longship, used for carrying passengers and cargo

LATEEN RIGGED Equipped with one or more triangular sails on a short mast; derived from the word "Latin" by Northern Europeans visiting the Mediterranean region

LATITUDE (see also LONGITUDE) Position to the north or south on the earth's surface, measured in degrees north or south of the equator. On a globe, latitude is shown in parallels (imaginary lines running east to west).

LODESTONE (see also COMPASS) Naturally magnetic iron oxide – used by early explorers when navigating at sea because of its north-pointing characteristic; discovered by the Chinese about 2,000 years ago. Lodestone was also used to magnetize compass needles.

LOGBOOK A record of a ship's voyage kept by the captain; usually included the ship's direction, speed and distance traveled, and any events on board ship, such as sickness among the crew or sightings of land or other ships

LONGITUDE (see also LATITUDE) Position to the east or west on the earth's surface. On a globe, longitude is shown in meridians (imaginary lines running north to south), which divide the earth into 360 degrees. Longitude is measured in degrees east or west from a known starting point – the meridian running through Greenwich, England. Every fifteen degrees of longitude is equal to one hour's difference in local time.

Cartographer

Jade carving

LONGSHIP (see also KNARR) Long, narrow Viking ship, often used by warriors on raids but also used for long-distance travel

MATCHLOCK Gun with an early, simple firing mechanism in which an S-shaped lever was pressed down to force a match (or lighted wick) into a flashpan, which ignited the powder; used by early explorers; later replaced by the flintlock

MORION HELMET Type of lightweight open helmet often made of a single piece of steel, or two pieces joined at the top, with a broad brim and peak; popular in the mid-16th century with European soldiers

MYRRH Valuable bitter aromatic gum from the bark of a tree, used in perfume, incense, medicines, and to anoint the dead; an important part of Egyptian religious ceremonies

The *Santa Maria*

NAO Large sailing ship, bigger-bellied than a caravel, originally built as a merchant ship and used on many voyages of exploration to carry supplies and weapons; became the most popular European ship for trading, exploration, and warfare in the 16th century until replaced by the galleon. Northern Europeans called this type of ship a carrack.

NINA One of the three ships on Columbus's first voyage of discovery, along with the Pinta and the Santa Maria. Columbus returned to Spain in the Nina after the Santa Maria was wrecked.

NORTHEAST PASSAGE Northern route from Europe to China through the Arctic, first navigated by the Norwegian Nils Nordenskjold on a scientific expedition from 1878 to 1879

NORTHWEST PASSAGE Route through the Arctic seas, along the coast of North America, giving access to the East from Europe; finally navigated by Roald Amundsen from 1903 to 1906

POLE STAR A bright star almost at the north celestial pole (the point in the sky directly above the Earth's north pole), used by early navigators in the northern hemisphere to work out their position at sea; also called Polaris or the North Star

PORCELAIN Hard translucent pottery invented by the Chinese; historically very popular in Europe

QUADRANT (see also POLE STAR) An instrument for navigation shaped like a quarter circle with an attached plumbline (weighted string) used to determine the position of the sun and stars. The navigator lined up one of the quadrant's straight sides with the sun or the Pole Star, then read off the position of the plumbline, to work out the ship's approximate latitude.

SANTA MARIA (see also CARAVEL) A caravel from northern Spain; Columbus's flagship on his first voyage of discovery; wrecked off the West Indies in 1492

SCURVY Often fatal disease caused by lack of vitamin C, which is found in fresh fruit and vegetables; formerly the leading cause of death among sailors on long sea voyages

SEAMAN'S ASTROLABE (see also ASTROLABE) Navigational instrument used to calculate a ship's latitude. The navigator lined up a sighting rule at the center of a brass ring and used it to sight the sun or a star, then read off the angle from markings around the ring.

SEXTANT Navigational instrument invented in the 1700s as a more accurate way of measuring latitude than the cross-staff and backstaff. The navigator looked through a sighting tube and moved a bar until the sun and horizon were lined up in small mirrors, then read off the angle.

SILK ROAD One of the world's oldest trade routes, which ran about 4,300 miles (7,000 km) across China and Asia; used by merchants from around 500 B.C.E. for hundreds of years before gradually falling into decline

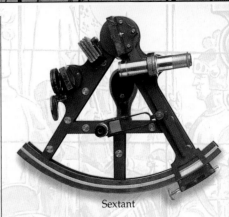

Sextant

SPICE ISLANDS European name given to islands in the Indian Ocean which produced valuable spices such as cinnamon

SQUARE RIGGED Equipped with a square sail suspended from a yard (a horizontal wooden beam) on a mast

TIMBUKTU Important trading center just south of the Sahara Desert in Africa; once the subject of many myths among Europeans

VELLUM A kind of fine parchment prepared from the skin of calves, kids, or lambs dipped in lime baths and burnished. Vellum was expensive, but held the ink better than ordinary hard parchment, and was therefore good for seafaring charts, which needed to be rolled and rerolled many times. Ordinary parchment was used for bound material, such as logbooks. Vellum and parchment were more widely available than paper.

VITTORIA A carrack; one of the five ships on Magellan's voyage to discover a route to Asia from the west (the others were the Concepción, the San Antonio, the Santiago, and the Trinidad); the only ship to complete the journey around the globe and home to Spain

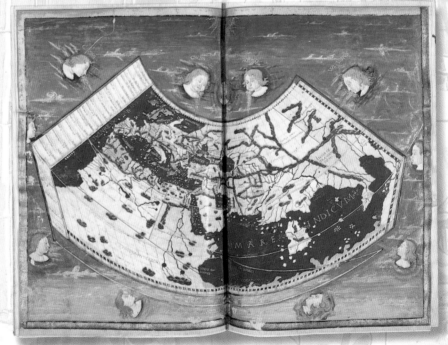

Map drawn on vellum

Index

A

Africa 10-11, 16, 18-21, 40, 46-47, 49, 66, 67
Alaska 34
Albert Lake, 47
Alexander the Great 10
Alvarado, Pedro de 30
America, 22-23, 33, 40, 42, 45, 58, 66, 67
Amundsen, Roald 40, 54, 65, 67
Anders, William 59
Antarctica 34, 44, 54-55
Arabs 9, 18-20, 29, 46
Arctic Ocean 41, 44, 50-53
Armstrong, Neil 58, 67
Asia, 8, 10-12, 16-18, 22, 46, 50, 66, 67
Assyrian Empire 7
Atlantic Ocean 6, 10, 12-13, 22, 24, 30, 48, 57, 64, 65, 66, 67
Audubon, John 45, 62
Australia 17, 24, 34-39, 49, 56, 67
Aztecs 30-33, 62

B

Baffin Island 40, 66
Baffin, William 66
Baker, Samuel 47
Ballard, Robert 67
Banks, Joseph 35, 49, 51
Barents, Willem 40, 66
Barth, Heinrich 67
Bates, Henry 48-49
Batutta, Ibn 19, 66
Bering, Vitus 67
Black Sea 10
Blaxland, John 38
Blériot, Louis 57
Bonaparte, Napoleon 42
Bonpland, Aimé 50
Bougainville, Louis 67
Botany Bay 38, 64
Britain 6, 10-12, 49
Burke, Robert 38, 63

Burton, Richard 46, 67
Byrd, Richard 55

C

Cabot, John 40, 63, 66
Cádiz 6
Calicut 20
California 44
Canada 42 44
Cape Horn 24
Cape of Good Hope 20-21, 24, 64, 66
Carthage 6
Cartier, Jacques 42, 66
Cavelier, Robert 43, 66
Central America 23, 33, 42
Champlain, Samuel de 42, 66
Cheng Ho 17
China 9, 16-19, 22, 30, 40
Clark, William 42, 45, 63, 64, 66, 66
Colorado 44
Columbia River 45
Columbus, Christopher 22-24, 26, 30, 63, 64, 71
Condamine, La 51, 67
Cook, Captain James 29, 34-38, 49, 51, 63, 64, 67, 68, 69
Cook Islands 15
Coronado, Francisco 33
Cortés, Hernando 30-31, 64, 66
Cousteau, Jacques 61, 67
Cunningham, Allan 50

D

Darwin, Charles 48-49, 67, 69
Diaz, Bartolomeu 2, 63, 64, 65, 66
Drake, Francis 66, 69, 70

E

Earhart, Amelia 56
East Africa 8, 17-18, 46
Egypt, 7-10 47
Elizabeth I, Queen 25, 40

England 13, 34, 36, 40
Ephesus 10
Erikson Leif, 12, 65
Erik the Red 12
Europe 10, 12-13, 16, 18, 22, 40
Eyre, Edward 67

F G

Ferdinand, King 22-23
Fiennes, Ranulph 67
Fiji 15, 34-35
Flinders, Matthew 38-39
Florida 32
France 11, 43
Franklin, John 40-41, 67
Frémont, John 44
Frobisher, Martin 40, 66
Gagarin, Yuri 58, 67
Gama, Vasco da 20, 63, 64, 66
Gibraltar 6
Grand Canyon 33
Great Dividing Range 38
Greenland 12-13, 57

H

Hartog, Dirk 38
Hatshepsut, Queen 8-9
Hawaiian Islands 34
Hedin, Sven 17
Henry the Navigator 20
Hooker, Joseph 50
Hormuz 17
Hudson, Henry 40-42, 66
Humboldt, Alexander 50, 67

I

Iceland 10, 12, 64
Incas 30-33
India 10, 17-20, 66
Indian Ocean 8, 18, 20, 25, 66
Indonesia 17-18, 20, 49
Indus River 10
Iraq 6-7
Isabella, Queen 22-23
Italy 11

J K

Japa 56
Jefferson, Thomas 42, 67
Johnson, Amy 56
Kansas River 33
Kenya 16
Khan, Emperor Kublai 17, 66
Kingsley, Mary 49

L

Lawson, William 38
Lebanon 6, 9
Lewis, Meriwether 42, 45, 63, 65, 67, 69
Lindbergh, Charles 57
Livingstone, David 19, 46-47, 63, 64, 67
Louisiana 42-43, 64

M

Macedonia 10
Mackenzie, Alexander 44, 63
Magellan, Ferdinand 24-25, 63, 64, 65, 66, 71
Malaya 21
Malta 6
Mayans 31
Mediterranean 6-7, 9, 11-14
Mexico 30-32
Missouri River 43, 45
Mongolia 19
Montreal 42
Moon 58-59

N O

Newfoundland 12-13, 40
Newport 40
New World 22-23, 33, 66
New York 40, 57
New Zealand 14, 34
Niger River 19
Nile 8, 10, 46-47, 67
North Africa 6, 8, 11, 18, 22

North America 12-13, 42-45, 62, 66, 67
North Pole 52-53, 55, 65, 67
Northeast Passage 66, 67
Northwest Passage 40-42, 66, 67
Norway 12-13
Oates, Lawrence 55
Oregon Trail 44

P

Pacific 14, 24-25, 29, 34-37, 45, 48-49, 51, 56, 66
Pakistan 10
Panama 23
Papua New Guinea 14
Park, Mungo 67
Parry, William 51, 53, 67
Peary, Robert 52, 63, 64, 65, 67
Persia 10, 17-18
Peru 30-32, 50
Philippines 20, 71
Phoenicians 6-7, 14, 65
Piccard, A. & J. 60, 67
Pike, Zebulon 44
Pizarro, Francisco 30, 32, 66
Platte River 44
Polo, Marco 16-17, 63, 65, 66
Polynesia 14-15, 35, 51
Portugal 20-21, 24
Przhevalsky, Nicolay 17

R

Raleigh, Walter 22
Romans 10-11
Ross, James 50, 67
Russia 57

S

St. Lawrence River 42
Sahara desert 10-11, 18-19, 22
Sardinia 6-7
Scandinavia 12
Scott, Robert 54-55, 65, 67, 69

Shackleton, Ernest 55, 67
Siebe, Augustus 60
Sierra Leone 20
Silk Road 16-17, 71
Somalia 8
Soto, Hernando de 32
South America 23-25, 30, 32-33, 42, 46, 49-51, 66
South Pole 54-55, 65, 67
Spain 6-7, 18, 23-25, 30, 32
Speke, John Hanning 46, 65, 67
Spice Islands 9, 20, 24, 30, 40, 66, 71
Stanley, Henry 46-47, 63, 64, 67
Stuart, John 38, 67
Sturt, Charles 38, 67

T

Tahiti 35
Tanganyika, Lake 46-47
Tasman, Abel 34, 63, 66
Tasmania 39
Thames River 13
Timbuktu 19, 67, 71
Tunis 6
Turkey 10
Tyre 7

U V

Veracruz 30
Verrazano, Giovanni da 40
Vespucci, Amerigo 23, 64
Victoria, Lake 46
Vikings 12-13, 40, 65, 66

W Z

Wallace, Alfred 48-49
Warburton, Peter 38
Wentworth, William 38
West Africa 6, 21, 49, 67
West Indies 22-23, 30
Wilkes, Charles 44
Wills, John 38, 63
Wright brothers 56
Zambezi River 47

Acknowledgments

The publisher would like to thank:
Caroline Roberts, Robert Baldwin, and Peter Ince of the National Maritime Museum, Greenwich; Joe Cribb, Simon James, Rowena Loverance, Carole Mendelson, Ann Pearson, James Puttnam, Jonathan N. Tubb, and Sheila Vainker of the British Museum; Anthony Wilson, Eryl Davies, Peter Fitzgerald, and Doug Millard of the Science Museum; Sarah Posey of the Museum of Mankind; Oliver Crimmen, Mike Fitton, and Roy Vickery of the Natural History Museum; the Royal Geographical Society; the Royal Botanical Gardens, Kew; the Peabody Museum of Salem, Mass.; the Bathseda Baptist Church Museum and the Gallery of Antique Costume and Textiles; Thomas Keenes, Christian Sévigny, and Liz Sephton for design assistance; Claire Gillard, Bernadette Crowley, and Céline Carez for editorial assistance; Jacquie Gulliver for her initial work on the book and Jane Parker for the index.

The publishers would also like to thank Peter Chrisp for his help on the revised edition.

Picture credits
The publisher would like to thank the following for their kind permission to reproduce their photographs:
(a=above, c-center, b=below, l-left, r=right, t=top)

The Art Archive: British Library 70bl.
Barnaby's Picture Library: 25tr.
Bridgeman Art Library London/New York: 18tl, 22br, 40tr; Academie des Sciences, Paris, France 66bl; Alecto Historical Editions/British Museum 64c; Bibliotheca Estense, Modena, Italy 71br; Bodleian Library, Oxford 40bl; British Library 64 cla, 64-65; British Museum 41tc; Hudson Bay Company 41bl; Metropolitan Museum of Art, New York 66tr; Private Collection 71cl; Royal Geographical Society 42tl, 42cl; Victoria & Albert Museum 45bl, 62tr; Yale Center for British Art, Paul Mellon Collection, USA 68cra; Brierley Hill Glass Museum, Dudley 48cr; Scott Polar Research Institute, Cambridge 53c.
British Museum, London: 9c.
Corbis: Leonard de Selva 66br; Macduff Everton 69tl; Peter Turnley 67br.
Endeavour Trust: Steve Wenban 68bl.
Mary Evans Picture Library: 6tl, 8tr, 10tl, 17br, 19tc, 19tr, 19cr, 24tr, 26tr, 27tr, 28tr, 29c, 38tl, 38tr, 38cr, 40cr, 42tr, 49c, 50cr, 55br, 56tr, 56br, 58tr, 60tl, 60br, 64tr, 67cl.
Getty Images: Hugh Sitton 68–69; Margarette Mead 65cl.

Robert Harding Picture Library: 2br, 11tr, 14bc, 15bl, 18c, 21tc, 21tr, 22cr, 27br, 30cl, 30–1, 35cr, 45c, 45cr, 46cl, 47tr, 47bl, 48bl, 50tr, 51tl, 57tr, 59tr, 62bc.
© **Michael Holford:** 6br, 7c, 70br.
Hulton–Deutsch: 12tl, 17cl, 20tl, 39tr, 56c, 57bl, 58cl.
Mansell Collection: 14tl, 21bl, 34cr.
Museu de Marinha, Lisbon: 20br.
NMAH/SI/Kim Nielsen 45br; NMNH/SI/Chip Clark 44tl.
National Maritime Museum, London: 34br, 34tl, 35bl, 40cl, 66–67.
The Natural History Museum, London: 69ca.
Nature Picture Library: L&M Dickinson 65 tr.
Peter Newark's Pictures: 43tr, 44br, 44c, 44cl.
By kind permission of the Trustees of the Parham Estate: 34bl.
Peabody Museum of Salem, Mass.:
Mark Sexton 26c, 26bl, 26–7c; Harvard University, Photo Hillel Burger 44–5.
Planet Earth Pictures: Flip Schulke 61c, 61br; Brian Coope 61bc.
Popperfoto: 54tl, 55tc.
Rex Features: 69bl.
Royal Geographical Society: Ranulph Fiennes 67tc; 71tl.
Science Photo Library: 59cr.
Syndication International: Front jacket bl, 2bl; Library of Congress, Washington DC 10bl; Nasjonal-gallerict, Oslo 12bl, 16tl; Bibliotèque Nationale, Paris 17bl; British Museum, London

20bl, 23tc, 24cl, 24bc, 30tl, 30bl; National Maritime Museum, London, 34br, 40cl; National Gallery of Art, Washington DC 43bl; Missouri Historical Society 45tr, 46tr, 46bc, 49bc; John Hancock Mutual Life Assurance Co. Boston, Mass. 52tl, 63tl.
Werner Forman Archive: 64bl.

Additional photography: Dave King, Colin Keates (pp. 50–53), Mark Sexton (pp. 26–27)
Maps: Sallie Alane Reason

Jacket credits:
Front: Tcr: National Geographical Society, UK; Tr: National Maritime Museum, UK. *Back:* Robert Harding Picture Library (clb); Natural History Museum (bc); National Maritime Museum (c, tl, tr); Royal Geographic Society (bl); Science Museum (br).

Every effort has been made to trace the copyright holders and we apologize in advance for any unintentional omissions. We would be pleased to insert the appropriate acknowledgment in any subsequent edition of this publication.

All other images © Dorling Kindersley For further information see:
www.dkimages.com